THE SPIRITUAL FEMINIST

Part devotional, part grimoire and part empowerment manual, *The Spiritual Feminist* offers readers her-stories, anecdotes and correspondences for dozens of goddesses. A wise, accessible and often irreverent guide, author Amythyst Raine-Hatayama reveals the Goddess in us all, showing women of all ages how to honor, embody and invoke Her many facets. Once I began reading *The Spiritual Feminist*, I couldn't stop. The feeling of understanding, and being understood, forged an intimate connection to the Goddess — riveting me to the page — stirring spiritual yearnings and opening new ways of seeing Her... almost as if for the first time.

Janet Boyer, Amazon.com Hall of Fame Reviewer, PaganSquare Sacred Symbols blogger and author of *Back in Time Tarot, Naked Tarot, 365 Tarot: Daily Meditations* and other titles

I'm not sure if you know or not but in September I had a heart attack and open heart surgery, and with the recovery process, I became a little depressed. Your book came to me at the perfect time, because reading it really lifted my spirits and gave me back my womanhood. The Information on the Goddesses of different belief systems is very interesting, and the personal life experiences, with the added touch of your "Craft", makes this book very inspiring for women.

Melita Kim Foster-Yates Truitt (Mystikal Melita) owner of Witchy Wisdom Network, witchywisdom.ning.com

The Spiritual
Feminist

The Spiritual
Feminist

Amythyst Raine-Hatayama

MOON
BOOKS

Winchester, UK
Washington, USA

First published by Moon Books, 2015
Moon Books is an imprint of John Hunt Publishing Ltd., Laurel House, Station Approach,
Alresford, Hants, SO24 9JH, UK
office1@jhpbooks.net
www.johnhuntpublishing.com
www.moon-books.net

For distributor details and how to order please visit the 'Ordering' section on our website.

Text copyright: Amythyst Raine-Hatayama 2014

ISBN: 978 1 78279 969 6

All rights reserved. Except for brief quotations in critical articles or reviews, no part of this
book may be reproduced in any manner without prior written permission from the publishers.

The rights of Amythyst Raine-Hatayama as author have been asserted in accordance with the
Copyright, Designs and Patents Act 1988.

A CIP catalogue record for this book is available from the British Library.

Design: Lee Nash

Printed in the USA by Edwards Brothers Malloy

We operate a distinctive and ethical publishing philosophy in all
areas of our business, from our global network of authors to
production and worldwide distribution.

CONTENTS

This book is dedicated to the goddesses within my ancestral lineage:
Lu Raine, Alpha, Tracy, Ruby, Bonny, Darlene, Georgia, Judy.

I would also like to thank my husband Joe for his support and
encouragement through this ridiculous process called "writing".

To my children, seven magickal individuals, for the inspiration they
are: Carrie, Anne, John, Beth, Laura, Sara, Emma.

And to my step-children, united with me through their father on this
journey called "Life": Brandon and Nicole.

Hail Mother Goddess

Hail Mother Goddess, full of grace;
Your consort is with You.
Blessed art thou among humanity.

And blessed is your creation –
Mother Earth and Father Sky,
And all that dwell within.

Mother Goddess, creatrix of the world,
Be with us now and throughout all incarnations.

Blessed Be

So many people throughout my life have told me who I am, what I must do, what I can't do, what I have to complete, and what I will never be able to accomplish... and then I met the Goddess.
Amythyst Raine-Hatayama

Preface

The only appealing part of Catholicism for me was the Virgin Mary. I know now that this was a natural attraction to the Goddess, the Divine Feminine. It was also a protective mechanism, a flinching away from the hard and fast patriarchal control and power of the male priests around me and their insistence on keeping all things feminine in what they thought of as a proper perspective, i.e. in its place according to their doctrine. Looking back, I can see that the nuns were also inexplicably and totally transfixed by this iconic female figure, though I don't think they totally understood their own fixation. They spent a great deal of time emphasizing and re-emphasizing the fact that the father, son, and holy ghost were "divine", but Mary was not.

Poor Mary, a humble human, impregnated out of wedlock, married off to Joseph, a gallant man praised for his merciful attitude to take on this mess in order to help out a woman who would be stoned to death for her condition, were it to become public knowledge. Poor Mary… "Big wheels keep on turnin'; Proud Mary keep on burnin'…"[1]

The father of her unborn illegitimate child was revealed to the world as the God of all creation, inspired and egged-on by his androgynous sidekick, the holy ghost; and together they conspire to keep Mary right where they want her, at the bottom of the spiritual totem pole, a useful vessel, a walking womb, an attractive and appealing incubator, and a publicist's dream.

In the end, they underestimated the power and strength of feminine spirituality; they underestimated the ingrained ancestral instinct to embrace matriarchal divinity. At the end of the day, the spiritual icon left to walk the red carpet is a little Jewish woman with her own set of prayer beads and a kick ass attitude.

Baby, the Goddess is back.

Part 1

Meet the Goddess

In almost every culture all over the world, there is evidence of matriarchal divinity and goddess worship. She is known by a myriad of names, across every cultural border and boundary you can think of, through a slew of ancient myths and legends, through written history, by word of mouth, and rough carvings on cave walls. There is no mistaking that once, long ago, the world bowed its head in reverence to the Mother Goddess.

I remember the first time this fact was revealed to me in all its shocking and wonderful glory. I was a teenager and still living with my grandmother at the time. She had recently subscribed to cable television. I was watching some program that I can't recall the name of, but I'll never forget the content. They were discussing ancient civilizations in terms of society and spirituality, and this voice suddenly stated: *"In the ancient world, it wasn't the God who was worshipped, it was the Goddess."* It was like a lightning bolt struck my reality, and I remember jerking myself upright in surprised shock and revelation, riveted by the idea. It was like coming home.

If you haven't already met the Goddess, I think it's time for an introduction; and if you're already acquainted, you'll rediscover some truths and revelations, as one always does with divinity. I've chosen forty-five of my favorite goddesses from across a wide variety of cultures. This is only a proverbial drop in the bucket, as far as a listing of goddesses goes. These are some of my favorites, some whom I've invoked over the years for inspiration, revitalization, magic, protection, and just because the energy felt good. Pay attention to the aspects of each divine name listed here; her particular energies, her specialties, the areas of your life that she can help you with. Listen to her story, feel her magic, open your heart and mind to the Feminine Divine, and draw into yourself her wisdom and power. "Her Story" is not just a mythical tale of the Goddess. It's *our* story, our voice.

Airmed

Her Story

Airmed is an Irish goddess of healing, witchcraft, and magic. This goddess is most noted for healing those who have fallen in battle. Airmed could be called the patron goddess of the green witch and herbalist, for as the myth goes, when her jealous father murdered her brother Miach, Airmed wept over his grave, and from her tears sprouted the healing herbs now found upon the earth. However, her father lashed out once more, throwing to the wind those healing herbs that Airmed had so carefully gathered in her cloak. Thus, the healing herbs of the world were scattered to the four corners, and for this reason it's said that no single individual will ever know all the secrets of these plants.

A pinch of this, a pinch of that, a leaf of sage, a leaf of mint, a petal from the rose, and so it goes and goes and goes: green witchcraft. This is the ultimate practice in cottage (or "kitchen") witchery. It brings to mind the stereotypical image of the witch gathering herbs, a basket over one arm, a sharp knife (her boline) in the other hand, murmuring to herself, leaving a blessing with each plant and the nature fairies connected to it in the form of a silver coin, sacred words, a gentle touch. The green witch is going to use the herbs she's so carefully collected to create oils and other magickal potions, bent over her steaming cauldron of brew, dried herbs hanging from the kitchen ceiling in an array of color and scent.

How many people feel the "magick" within flowers, herbs, wild flowers (aka weeds), but they don't fully understand just what it is they feel or why? Why are some individuals drawn to a favorite flower? What's your favorite flower? Look up its magickal properties, and you may be very surprised at the connection. There's a bit of the green witch in us all, deep inside, buried with all the other dormant ancient knowledges and practices of our ancestors. It's time to open this door, to reconnect with nature. It is magick waiting to happen in the form of infinite possibilities.

Embracing the Goddess

During these times of modern conflict and battle, embrace the goddess Airmed by invoking her energy for protection and healing to those men and women serving in the armed forces.

Airmed's Correspondences

Herbs: Patchouli, mugwort, bittersweet

Animal: Eagle (American soldiers). Note: when invoking Airmed's energy for healing warriors, call upon the animal energy, the totem, that is connected with your country.

Colors: Green, pink

Planet: Earth (Gaia)

Day: Sunday, Friday

Element: Earth

Feminine Face: Mother

Symbols: Sword, battle gear, plants and greenery

Aphrodite

Her Story

Aphrodite is the "Goddess of the Sea", the Greek goddess of love and war, which at first sounds conflicted, yet there are similar elements to each. This is the goddess of both marriage and illicit affairs, her energy geared to the passions found within both. She is also recognized as the goddess of battles and wars, and in this too is an irony, as romantic relationships can often contain these elements as well as the more conventional and desired emotions. Aphrodite is the epitome of physical beauty and pleasure.

What is true beauty, and whose yardstick are we measuring ourselves by? Just how idealistic has our culture, our society, become? Is our obsession with youth connected to our cultural view of what's beautiful – and what's not? Why do we view elderly people, particularly women, as ugly? Is this why the Fashion Lords feel compelled to label clothes "age appropriate", so elderly women are kept covered, so we don't view their wrinkled skin and aging bodies? And why is it that other cultures don't seem to reflect this repulsion for older women?

In African communities that are naturally sparsely dressed, you see all ages (men and women) with exposed bodies, and everyone appears to be accepted as is; in fact, no one seems to give it a second thought. We are a vain, youth-obsessed, perfection-driven society. The only way that this stigma can be broken is if women stand up and be heard; shed light on this issue, unite, and make some noise.

It's time to reclaim the term "beauty", to redefine it, to embrace womanhood – in all of its ages and stages – as beautiful, magickal, and miraculous.

Embracing the Goddess

Invoke Aphrodite when you need more self-confidence in yourself, in your personal appearance; when you need assistance with romantic relationships or disputes. Call upon this goddess for love spells, spells of beauty and youth; call upon this goddess when romantic energy is desired and the flames of passion need some fanning. Expect her response to be swift and sometimes unexpected.

Aphrodite's Correspondences

Herbs: Apple, rose, catnip

Animal: Dove

Color: Red, pink, green

Planet: Venus

Day: Friday

Element: Water

Feminine Face: Maiden

Symbol: Mirror

Arianrhod

Her Story

Arianrhod is a Welsh moon goddess. She rules not only the moon, but the stars and sea as well. She's often referred to as "The Silver Wheel of the Sea". This is a goddess of prophecy and dreams, and it's her energy that is desired for divination by seers and psychics. Arianrhod is also the ruler of reincarnation, karma, and magical realms. She radiates feminine authority and feminine power. A time keeper of the universe, Arianrhod is one of the five goddesses of Avalon, the legendary island inhabited by priestesses who serve the Mother Goddess.

The woman entered the grove with a sense of grace and quiet composure. She walked slowly and carefully through the trees, silently, with only the occasional whisper of her breath or a barely audible footfall. She walked through the grove until she saw that which she was seeking: a silver pool of light filtering through the trees, filling a small clearing ahead. Lifting her arm, she gently brushed aside the branches of a young maple tree and stepped into the clearing, into the brilliant glow of the full moon.

The woman reached for the clasp at her neck, and the long robe she was wearing dropped to her feet, leaving her to bathe within the silver light in naked splendor, her body energized by the moon's ethereal glow.

Standing straight and tall, her feet slightly apart, the priestess raised her arms before the moon and began to invoke upon herself its energy, to draw down within herself the magic of the moon and the power of the Goddess.

Embracing the Goddess

Call upon Arianrhod for second sight, to enhance your already natural female intuition. Call upon Arianrhod when you need to see that which cannot be seen in any natural way. This goddess will also lend her powerful and graceful energy to esbats, reveling in the magic of the moon and the priceless spirituality found within.

Arianrhod's Correspondences

Herbs: Apple, catnip, lilac, raspberry, strawberry
Animal: Owl
Color: Blue, silver
Planet: Moon
Day: Monday
Element: Water
Feminine Face: Mother
Symbol: Moon

Artemis

Her Story

Artemis is known as "The Virgin Huntress", a Greek goddess of the hunt. She personifies independence, strength, and the warrior within each of us. She protects young girls until the age of marriage, defends those who are weak, and is said to be a protectress to those women enduring childbirth. Her energy is pure of intention, yet incredibly strong, not for the faint of heart.

Women can be weak because we're told we are. Don't believe everything everyone tells you. Deep inside every woman is a rich well of strength that might lie dormant until life's circumstances trigger this dragon, until there is a need, an urgency, for the warrior within her to rise to the surface. It will happen in the spark of a moment; it will be like putting a flame to a stick of dynamite; it will be explosive, miraculous, amazing, and significant to everyone connected to this woman and to this woman herself.

Know that there is a warrior within you. Know that you are so much stronger than anyone tells you; stronger even than you think. Know that nothing and no one can dominate you, that you are in control of your destiny. Know that you are a supreme being, complete within yourself, independent, trail-blazing, competent, and awe-inspiring. Live your life in a manner that honors the warrior goddess within.

Embracing the Goddess

Call upon Artemis for courage, strength, and protection, especially protection of maidens... for yourself, your daughters, your nieces, your granddaughters. As she exudes the essence of independence and individualism, so she will teach you to embrace these attributes within yourself.

Artemis's Correspondences

Herbs: Wood sorrel, barley, patchouli, primrose

Animal: Deer, bear

Color: Green, brown

Planet: Earth

Day: All seven

Element: Earth

Feminine Face: Maiden

Symbol: Bow and arrow

Astarte

Her Story

Astarte is the Mesopotamian goddess of love and war. This might, at first, seem oddly conflicting, but on reflection there are more similarities than differences. Her name literally means "star" and she is the companion and the power behind the moon. Astarte is considered queen of both the morning and evening stars, Venus and Mercury.

She rules the spirits of the dead. As a love goddess, the energies she influences include sexual experiences, physical passion, marriage, female sensuality, and feminine independence. As a warrior goddess she influences battles, conflicts, and victories.

After fifteen years of marriage and six children, I was sitting in the courtroom during our divorce proceedings when my soon-to-be ex-husband's attorney pointed a finger in my direction and said to the judge, "She's unemployable."

How crushing were those words in the face of the fact that I would soon be reckoning with the daunting responsibility of supporting a large family on my own. Already panicked by the idea, aware of the fact that the last fifteen years as a housewife left me with virtually no work history or references, this comment was a like a final blow to my self-confidence.

But this callous remark, passed off with such finality, did something else – it made me angry.

Deep within the center of me, hidden by the housewife and mother, lay something that had been dormant and repressed for a very long time. Deep within me, the warrior goddess was stirring, coming to, blinking her eyes in the bright light of necessity, shaking the sleep and cobwebs from her wits. She stood unsteadily to her feet and, as she did so, the earth trembled, the trees shook, the sky darkened.

The warrior goddess was ready to do battle, ready to beat the odds, ready to prove her adversaries wrong. She was ready to build upon her strengths, to cash in on her intelligence, to flex her muscles in the arena of life. The warrior goddess was ready to take on the world... and succeed.

Embracing the Goddess

Women can invoke the goddess Astarte when they are fighting to reclaim their independence, when they are seeking to explore the intimate side of their femininity, when they are in need of strength, direction, purpose, and a touch of the warrior spirit. Know that within each gentle feminine soul, there resides a steely and daunting heroine just waiting to be awoken. Call upon her when you need her.

Astarte's Correspondences

Herbs: Bay, clove, marigold, hyssop (Fire), apple, calamus, hibiscus, thyme (Water)

Animal: Dove

Color: Yellow, pink, green

Planet: Mercury, Venus

Day: Tuesday, Friday

Element: Fire, Water

Feminine Face: Maiden

Symbol: Sphinx, star

Athene

Her Story

Athene is the Greek goddess of wisdom, considered the "Wise Warrior", able to temper the fighting spirit with balance, a sense of purpose, and ethics. She was not born from a mother's womb, but it's said instead that she was fully formed from the head of Zeus and came into being wearing battle armor.

Why do so many of the goddesses encompass the spirit of a warrior? Why? Athene reminds us that not all battles are won with brawn, but by intelligence, patience, quiet fortitude, and perseverance. However, do not underestimate her.

"We can do this the easy way, or we can do this the hard way," says Athena.

And the best implication here: *We can do this.*

Where does your strength come from? What is it that runs through your veins that is reminiscent of your ancestors? Within each of us lies a personal lineage rich in history, culture, and tradition. Who am I? Who am I – really? For many of us, these answers will come easy; but for others, it will require an effort to seek and search out, through mists of time perhaps, the answer to such a simple question... *Who am I?*

Sometimes knowing where you came from is just as important as knowing where you're headed.

Embracing the Goddess

Immersed as we are in feminine physical bodies, tied as we are to our fathers, their names, and their reputations; we can become as warriors when the inclination and the need arise. Call on Athene when you wish to delve into your personal history, when you wish to study and search out your forebears. Call upon Athene when it's raw bold energy that's needed, when delicacy is put on the back burner, and you need to kick some ass, whether figuratively or literally.

Athene's Correspondences

Herbs: Cloves, allspice, holly, wormwood, ginger
Animal: Owl
Color: Red, orange
Planet: Mars
Day: Tuesday
Element: Fire
Feminine Face: Maiden
Symbols: Olive tree

Aurora

Her Story

Aurora is the Roman goddess of dawn, and as the dawn brings us a fresh new day, so Aurora brings us light and renewal. It's said that Aurora holds the power to open the gates of heaven, thus allowing her brother Sol, the sun, to travel across the sky. Her children are the four winds and the constellations, reaffirming Aurora's connection to the heavens. This goddess grants rejuvenation. She also possesses the wonderful power to wash away our deeds and misfortunes, granting us a clean slate on which fresh beginnings can be made.

I will honor Aurora by calling on her children, the four winds, knowing that her energy comes with them:

North Wind:
Bring with you a breath of fresh air in the form of common sense, a quiet will, the ability to stand steadfast in the face of calamity. Connect me to the physical realm, to the element of Earth, that I may experience its joy and appreciate its beauty.

East Wind:
Bring with you a breath of fresh air in the form of intelligence, curiosity, a willingness to learn new things, the chance for a new beginning, and the miracle of transformation. Connect me to the mental realm, the element of Air, that my mind may grow and expand, that I continue to learn throughout my life, that I will be ripe with new ideas and amazing revelations.

South Wind:
Bring with you a breath of fresh air to banish those things in life that are halting my progress, to throw light on the

darkness of deception, to renew vitality and vigor. Connect me to the element of Fire to fan the flames of passion in my life; passion for a cause, passion for my lover, passion for life.

West Wind:
Bring with you a breath of fresh air to heal body, mind, and spirit; to cleanse my soul and clear my space; to make fertile anything in my life that will benefit from fertility; to make heard that inner voice that guides me. Connect me to the element of Water to bring me dreams; prophetic dreams, dreams to bring messages from the dead, dreams to enlighten me through my spirit guides.

Embracing the Goddess

We all have regrets in life. Aurora allows us to find relief from these regrets, setting the energy right, allowing us to move forward with our lives, to try again, to make amends, to move on. Remember: a new dawn means a new day, which means a second chance.

Aurora's Correspondences

Herbs: Fennel, lavender, marjoram, eyebright
Animal: Bird, butterfly
Color: Yellow, blue
Planet: Mercury
Day: Wednesday
Element: Air
Symbol: Feathers, aurora borealis

Baba Yaga

Her Story

Baba Yaga is a Russian goddess, an ancient witch and "Mistress of Magick". She dwells in the forests, so it's said, and for those brave enough to tread through the woods, or those brave enough to invoke this hag goddess, she will answer one question that you put to her.

Baba Yaga highlights the shadow side of life, all of those dark places conventional society says we should avoid; yet in truth, all those places we must investigate and explore in order to learn our life lessons and to grow and mature as women. This goddess controls time and the four elements. She is the keeper of wisdom and she controls the spirits.

Imagine being able to ask the Divine one question and receive an answer. What would your question be? What is it you seek from the answer?

Using the correspondences listed on page 18, set up an altar to honor and to invoke Baba Yaga. Write your question on a slip of paper and offer it to her, knowing that you *will* receive an answer.

Allow Baba Yaga to connect with the Crone in you... She's there, you know, no matter what your age; she's there, waiting in the shadows to dispense wisdom, to celebrate life's lessons, to lead the way on this incredible journey called Life.

Embracing the Goddess

Modern society avoids the Crone, often viewing her as ugly and frightening. She is anything but. The Crone aspect of the Goddess is rich with wisdom that can only come from experience and maturity. She is beautiful when depicted as the hag, every line and wrinkle a story. She is a teacher and mentor to young women and women in the midst of motherhood and life. The Crone is the shadow side of the Goddess that we need to embrace. She does not represent the end of our journey; she represents completion and accomplishment.

Baba Yaga's Correspondences

Herbs: Absinthe, mugwort, skullcap, sage

Animal: Raven

Color: Black

Planet: Moon (the waning crescent)

Day: All seven

Element: Earth, Air, Fire, Water

Feminine Face: Crone

Symbol: Mortar and pestle

Bast

Her Story

Bast is the Egyptian cat goddess known as the "Mother of Cats". She's often depicted as a graceful woman with the head of a cat. She's also known as the "Goddess of the Ointment Jar", the creator of perfumes and oils, and it's definitely her energy that will aide you in the preparation of such, including magical oils.

This is another Egyptian goddess credited with being a guardian of the household, a protectress of women and children. Bast's energies are also connected to the moon and sunrise, anointing (of course, the oils), health and prosperity, love, fertility, sensuality, and music.

Cats: The Magical Creatures Behind the Goddess

In the first place, they usually come to you, you don't acquire them; and if you happen to, they may disappear quickly, quietly, and mysteriously; leaving hardly a trace that allows you to remember they were ever there.

They return like actions for like actions, like emotions for like emotions. If you are cruel, they will return this action in kind, with the grasp of a jaw, or the swiping rake of a claw. If you are gentle, so shall they be, calmly and matter-of-factly washing your hand or your cheek as they would one of their own kind, showing in their own way their acceptance of you – in spite of your human condition. Oh joy, you are considered worthy!

Human outbursts are generally met with two reactions, either a quick departure that speaks of not only fear, but also severe disapproval, or an intense stare of disdain, which speaks of superiority and quiet wisdom. They refuse to remain in the company of one who would wish them ill. They refuse to remain in the company of one who offends their senses. They are what they are, and they do as they do, and in the process they cross paths with the human race and our wearisome state of being. They know, they figured us out long ago.

Embracing the Goddess

My household is a household filled with cats and cat energies. The essence of Bast is called upon here for a variety of magic: for protection, both for our cats and for the humans who inhabit this house, as well as during the preparation of magical oils. There is a mystery to this animal that hints of old magic and ancient ways. Embrace the wisdom you see in the eyes of a cat, knowing that this goddess is close by.

Bast's Correspondences

Herbs: Catnip, mint, allspice, dragon's blood
Animal: Cat
Color: Red, orange
Planet: Mars
Day: Tuesday (cat magic)
Element: Water, Fire
Feminine Face: Maiden
Symbol: Sistrum

Baubo

Her Story

Baubo is the Greek goddess of laughter and music. She has the ability to release inhibitions, to unleash the bawdy side within us all, to sexually liberate the most stuffed of stuffed shirts. Baubo is the spirit of laughter and merriment. She offers us the wonderful liberation that is freedom from judgment. In Demeter's time of sorrow, when her daughter Persephone was abducted, Baubo attempted to lift Demeter's sadness and depression with music, so the myth goes.

Freedom from judgment: some people have no idea how constrictive, how oppressive, how debilitating this can be, to be judged by other people, to be held up to someone else's yardstick of success or propriety.

Invoke Baubo to break the chains that bind. Invoke Baubo to rediscover your own worth, your own potential. Invoke Baubo to discover your inner strength, your inner wisdom, your personal power and magic.

So many people throughout my life have told me who I am, what I must do, what I can't do, what I have to complete, and what I will never be able to accomplish... *and then I met the Goddess.*

Embracing the Goddess

When dark and gloomy surroundings, circumstances, or people are weighing you down, invoke Baubo to lighten the tone, to release pent-up energies. This is the goddess who will help you let down your hair and loosen up; but be careful with her energy. Ask yourself just how loose you want to get.

Baubo's Correspondences

Herbs: Eyebright, star anise, slippery elm
Animal: Gooney birds
Color: Yellow
Planet: Mercury
Day: Wednesday
Element: Air
Feminine Face: Maiden
Symbol: Tambourine

Black Tara

Her Story

Black Tara is a Tibetan goddess of power, worshipped in both Hindu and Buddhist traditions. She reigns over willpower, and she has the uncanny ability to measure our actions to our motives, which is why you want to be very sure you have the purist of intentions when calling upon this goddess. Black Tara administers tests for the soul, determining our evolvement and our spiritual enlightenment. She rules over spirits, exorcisms, and healing of both the body and the mind.

Willpower: Black Tara, give me the strength and willpower to make healthy choices, healthy choices for body, mind, and spirit.

Motives: Black Tara, give me the wisdom and insight needed to see the truth in people, to find their shadow side, and to seek out the light.

Spiritual Enlightenment: Black Tara, lead me by the hand, down the path of the Goddess, that I may embrace Feminine Divinity in all its beauty and glory.

Spirits: Black Tara, introduce me to my spirit guide, that this spirit may be with me from this point on, to lead me, to guide me, to warn me, to protect me.

Healing: Black Tara, heal my body, that I might thrive and grow and enjoy the physical world; heal my spirit, that I may connect with the Divine and follow my destiny; heal my mind, that I will see clearly, love clearly, and grow in knowledge and wisdom.

Embracing the Goddess

Summon Black Tara when you are spiritually clearing and cleansing a space. Call upon this goddess when healing is in order, when you feel the need to clearly view someone else's intentions, when your willpower needs strengthening, and when you desire spirit contact.

Black Tara's Correspondences

Herbs: Cloves, garlic, henbane, wolf's bane
Animal: Raven
Color: Black
Planet: Saturn
Day: Saturday
Element: All four
Feminine Face: Mother
Symbol: Female Buddha

Blue Tara

This goddess is worshipped in both Hindu and Buddhist traditions. She is a goddess of liberation and is the ultimate goddess for women to call upon when they need help escaping a negative life situation. Her energy is used to cleanse negativity and to restore positive aspects to your life. Blue Tara is a protectress of women.

I am
I am strong
I am wise
I am a goddess

I am
I am capable
I am intuitive
I am a priestess

I am
I am gentle
I am responsible
I am a mother

I am
I am loving
I am faithful
I am a wife

I am
I am _____
I am _____
I am a _____

I Am!

Embracing the Goddess

Call upon the energy of Blue Tara when you are a mother, a wife, a daughter, a girlfriend, and you find your safety and wellbeing threatened by negative or abusive behavior. Blue Tara will wash away the source of this negativity, leaving the path open for you to escape, to find your way home, to discover a new road and a new destiny. This goddess will give you the courage and the strength to break the chains that bind.

Blue Tara's Correspondences

Herbs: Lemongrass, fennel, sage, anise, eyebright, slippery elm
Color: Yellow, blue
Planet: Mercury
Day: Wednesday
Element: Air
Feminine Face: Mother
Symbol: Full moon

Brighid

Her Story

Brighid is the Irish goddess of the Sacred Flame; often referred to as the "White Goddess", she is also another of the triple goddesses. Brighid rules the realms of poetry, healing, smithcraft, inventions, and craftsmanship. She is the "Keeper of the Holy Wells and Rivers", where many go to seek healing; she's also ruler of the "Sacred Flames of Creativity". Her festival is celebrated on February 2, called Imbolc, a celebration of the return of spring and fertility to the land.

For women across the board, for women coming out of the darkness, weathering the storm, to greet the sun, the blue sky, and a new age of fertility and personal growth, the magic and energy of Brighid will welcome you with open arms.

How many women out there feel hopelessly caught up in the dark places their lives have become? How many women out there have lost sight of the light, the meaning and purpose of their personal journey? As Brighid returns the world to springtime and fertility, so this ancient Irish goddess will return you to the path you were meant to travel, the journey you were meant to make. She will help you see the light, refocus, regain your personal sense of worth and wellbeing.

As Brighid bursts upon the world, dancing within the rays of golden sunshine, so shall you relearn the dance of life.

Embracing the Goddess

As Brighid heralds the return of the sun and a period of fertility to the earth, so can she imbue your life with renewed fertility, promise, and growth. Invoke this goddess and embrace her energy when you need a burst of creative influence, when you need the touch of a magical muse upon your shoulder, when you need inspiration from the ancient winds of time, when you're in need of healing, whether it be of mind, or body, or soul.

Brighid's Correspondences

Herbs: Basil, bay, celandine, benzoic

Animal: Lambs, ewes

Color: Blue, yellow, white

Planet: Sun

Day: Sunday

Element: Fire

Feminine Face: Maiden

Symbol: Sun, Brighid's Cross

Cailleach

Her Story

Called "The Scottish Hag", Cailleach is a blue-faced crone so close to death that her face is often portrayed in a skeletal form. She is also, ironically, considered the creatrix of nature – the wilderness, the landscape, and wild things in their most beautiful aspects.

This goddess is the personification of winter, and it's this season she dominates. It's said that Cailleach rams her staff into the ground, creating the three months of winter and the natural "death" of nature that is associated with it. She rules the time from Winter Solstice to Imbolc, when the Maiden Brighid will awaken the land to springtime, growth, and fertility.

Cailleach is the harbinger of our fears and death. Again, there is an irony to this goddess, in that she is also considered a great sorceress, a healer, and a midwife. But when you think about it, it may not be so ironic after all. Birth and death are the two biggest transitions that we face in life, and they are not so different. They're just two journeys headed in opposite directions.

Through the centuries women have been told in our male-dominated societies that they "can't". They can't do this, they're not strong enough to do that. Women have run the gauntlet of male-imposed restrictions over the course of history, from not being allowed to own land, not being allowed to have a voice in politics, not being allowed to hold certain jobs, and not being allowed to reach their full potential in endless arenas of life. A lot has changed, and there have been improvements, particularly in our western world, but this is not yet true for women on a global level.

Cailleach runs shrieking through the mists of time, hammer and staff in hand, to scream the truth... *You can! You can! You can!*

Remember this, her lesson. Take up your own hammer and staff, build your life, build your world, build your dreams, reach your goals and succeed. Succeed with all the fervor of this old Scottish hag in all her glory.

Embracing the Goddess

Women can and do accomplish tasks and reach goals that are overtly dominated by men in our society. Embrace Cailleach when you need the strength and stamina to break molds and forge new ground.

Cailleach's Correspondences

Herbs: Dandelion, eyebright, slippery elm, star anise
Animal: Wolves, deer
Color: Yellow
Planet: Mercury
Day: Wednesday
Element: Air
Feminine Face: Crone
Symbol: Hammer, staff

Ceres

Her Story

Ceres is the Roman goddess of agriculture and the mother of Proserpina. She influences the harvest (growth), motherhood, and fertility, as well as maternal love and responsibility.

The ancients explained springtime with the story of Ceres and the tremendous maternal love she had for her daughter. Ceres' daughter Proserpina was kidnapped by Pluto, a god of the underworld, to be his bride. Ceres was so outraged, and even more so after she learned that Proserpina's father Jupiter had given his approval, that she decided to roam the world of men disguised as an old hag, cursing the planting and harvests so that a famine ensued. Jupiter realized the only way to stop Ceres was to appease her and bring their daughter back, but it was too late. Proserpina had been given food by Pluto while in the underworld, and anyone who eats in the underworld will no longer be able to leave it behind; but Proserpina escapes for four months every year, and during this time the world flourishes with new growth, plants, grains, and harvest.

From springtime until harvest, Ceres is reunited with her beloved daughter.

I stand in the middle. On one side is my mother, on the other side is my oldest daughter. There are estrangements on both sides, the reasons petty and lost in time, hazy and forgotten, so long ago it was.

Why and how do family members cut each other off, particularly mothers and daughters? What links are broken, what connections lost? How do the bonds get cut; where do the feelings go; how does an individual suddenly, and without warning, simply stop acknowledging the existence of a family member?

As the goddess Ceres would not give up until her daughter was brought back to her, neither will I give up until my mother acknowledges me, establishes communication, and we find common ground on which to continue a relationship. Neither will I give up until my daughter and I are reunited, if not on the same page, at least within the same book.

Through the power and energy of this goddess, Ceres, through her example of tenacious love and devotion to her daughter, I cast the magick and light the candle for reconciliation.

The daughter deserves the attention and affection of her mother; the mother deserves the attention and affection of her daughter.

So mote it be.

Embracing the Goddess

For mothers who need to reconnect with their daughters, for daughters who need to reconnect with their mothers, invoke Ceres for success in these ventures. Invoke Ceres to amplify and radiate the undying love and devotion a mother has for her child, for her daughter. Invoke Ceres for fertility – physical fertility, as well as fertility and growth in other aspects of your life.

Ceres' Correspondences

Herbs: Barley, wheat, corn, buckwheat, rye
Color: Green, brown
Planet: Gaia (Earth)
Day: All seven
Element: Earth
Feminine Face: Mother
Symbols: Scepter, basket of fruit and flowers, grains

Cerridwen

Her Story

Cerridwen is the Welsh goddess who is most noted for her cauldron of transformation. She brews potions for divine inspiration and wisdom; and from the depths of this cauldron, all womankind will benefit. She also has the ability to disperse justice with a cold eye to mercy. Cerridwen is the ultimate queen of shape-shifting, transforming herself to meet the need, to confront a challenge, to survive a confrontation, able to render herself unrecognizable to an enemy.

One of the triple goddesses, Cerridwen is the Crone aspect, sharing the pedestal with her counterparts: Blodeuwedd (the Maiden) and Arianrhod (the Mother). She is a goddess of the moon, ruling prophecy, as well as the powers of death and rebirth.

A woman's life is in a constant state of transformation. From the moment we leave the womb we begin our journey through this mortal experience as someone's daughter, someone's sister, someone's wife, someone's mother. But in the course of this journey, when does the time come to shed all these titles and to discover the inner woman, who we really are, without the burden of other people's expectations? And how are women able to transition within these roles without losing their sense of identity completely?

This is where the energy of Cerridwen comes into play. We can learn from this goddess the secrets of complete transition; temporary transition; and transitions that are necessary for our survival; transitions that give us an advantage over an adversary, advantages over our own self-doubt, as well as the tools and expertise to take on new roles with confidence and success.

Embracing the Goddess

Invoke Cerridwen when you are challenged by life's varied roles, when you need special skills and talents to maneuver through an experience. Invoke this goddess when the desire within you for transformation is so powerful it cannot be ignored.

Cerridwen's Correspondences

Herbs: Gardenia, lily, lotus, moonwort, poppy
Animal: White sow
Color: Blue, silver
Planet: Moon
Day: Monday
Element: Water
Feminine Face: Crone
Symbol: Cauldron

Copia

Her Story

Copia is a Roman goddess of abundance, wealth, and the harvest. She's often depicted carrying a Horn of Plenty, known as a "cornucopia", filled with the bounty of the earth: grains and fruit. This goddess is celebrated with offerings of wine and food. The "Goddess of Plenty", she embraces abundance with enthusiasm.

In theory, everyone living in this nice, shiny, modern world should be rolling in plenty – plenty of food and clothes, and baubles and bling, plenty of opportunities for good healthcare, a nice home, a good education; but that is not the case. Our world is still divided between the haves and the have-nots. There are still serious issues that women of the world are facing, and it's time for women of the world to unite and even things out a bit.

Below are a variety of charities to think about. If you want to make a difference closer to home, consider starting a local charity in your neck of the woods... Women (and the Goddess) can make a difference:

1. Violence

V-Day: Ninety-three percent of its funding goes to programs. Active in 81 countries, V-Day works to end violence against women and girls. Its hallmark? The Vagina Monologues, put on by volunteers to raise funds for local antiviolence groups. In countries where shows aren't possible, V-Day gives grants for programs – such as the V-Day Safe House in Kenya, which helps girls escape female genital mutilation. V-Day has raised more than $30 million in eight years.
vday.org

2. Children

Save the Children: Ninety percent of funding goes to programs.
Ten million children under five die each year, including four million newborns. A critical goal of Save the Children is saving the lives of these infants in eighteen of the world's poorest countries by providing infant vaccinations and healthcare for pregnant women. Sponsor a child for $28 a month, or earmark your dollars for initiatives, like educating girls or providing microloans for women. Celeb moms Debra Messing, Courteney Cox, and Maria Bello showed their support through an eBay auction to benefit this nonprofit organization.
savethechildren.org

3. Women's Fund

Women's Funding Network: Eighty-five percent of its funding goes to programs.
Looking to help women, but not sure where to give? Consider WFN, a coalition of private and community foundations around the world. In the past twenty years, its 115 funds have given more than $200 million to a wide variety of women's and girls' organizations. How does it work? As with a mutual fund, you designate your money for the fund of your choice, then that fund distributes grants to smaller nonprofits. The best perk? WFN monitors each fund, so you don't have to.
fundforward.org

4. Workplace

National Partnership for Women and Families: Eighty-six percent of its funding goes to programs.
Sexually harassed at work? Afraid you'll lose your job because you're pregnant? There are now laws to protect you, thanks in part to the National Partnership. This group has fought for every major policy advancement that has helped women and

families in the past three decades. The group fights for national legislation, but can help individuals find resources needed for their own battles.

nationalpartnership.org

Embracing the Goddess

It was drummed into my head throughout Catholic parochial school the concept of poverty as a positive and spiritually uplifting state. Quite frankly, I don't find anything about poverty uplifting. It represents a constant struggle for survival, a constant struggle to take care of your children, to keep a home, to live a life with dignity and joy. Poverty sucks and I don't find one thing about it desirable or admirable in any way.

Neither would Copia.

Invoke this goddess and call upon her for the energy of abundance and fertility, wealth and hedonistic delight. Honor the goddess spirit in you that claims your right to all the good things in life.

Copia's Correspondences

Herbs: Oleander, patchouli, wheat, oats
Animal: Hamster, packrat, squirrel
Color: Green, brown
Planet: Earth
Day: All seven
Element: Earth
Feminine Face: Mother
Symbol: Cornucopia (Horn of Plenty)

Cybele

Her Story

Cybele is a Roman goddess, "Mother to the Gods", and the patron goddess of transsexuals and transgendered individuals, particularly males. Her ancient followers were ritually castrated transsexuals. She is the goddess of nature and fertility, presiding over caves and mountaintops. Cybele protects city dwellers from invaders and war.

When her husband, Attis, was castrated and died of his wounds, it was Cybele who resurrected him. She was celebrated with wild festivals of music and dancing, unabashed pagan enthusiasm, and orgies.

The goddess Cybele brings to me one word: tolerance.

If tolerance is to manifest in the world, it must be accompanied by education, understanding, empathy, and love. A human being's sexuality and spirituality are things that cannot be cubby-holed. Our western culture, modern as we like to think we are, is severely restrained and judgmental in both of these departments, particularly in certain areas of the United States, and absolutely in certain mid-Eastern countries.

It's okay to be gay, it's okay to be transgendered, transsexual, or any other sexual orientation. It's okay to be pagan, it's okay to follow natural earth-based religions, or indigenous forms of spirituality, or to follow nothing at all. It's okay not to be Christian (or Jewish, or Muslim). It's okay not to be straight.

It's all okay... really, it is.

People are terrified and panicked by something that they don't understand, or something that they misunderstand. They are flummoxed by anything that is different, or anything that they have been conditioned to view as wrong or evil. It's time to shine a light on the world and accept every individual as a unique and glorious being.

Embracing the Goddess

As Cybele protected ancient cities from the onslaught of invasion and destruction from enemies, so she can be invoked today to protect our metropolitan areas from the threat of terrorists. Invoke this goddess and take advantage of her power to shield us from terrorist attacks.

For those people living in the world as transsexuals or trans-gendered individuals, this is the goddess to call upon for protection and for the celebration of your unique individuality and the ability to live your life true to yourself, in peace and harmony with the rest of the world.

Cybele's Correspondences

Herbs: Hemp, pansy, skullcap, lady's slipper
Animal: Chameleon
Color: Black, rainbow
Planet: Saturn
Day: Saturday
Element: Earth
Feminine Face: Mother
Symbol: Mountains, rainbows, the peace sign

Demeter

Her Story

Demeter is the Greek goddess of the harvest, considered "Mother of the Harvest". This agricultural goddess, credited for bringing the knowledge of plowing and sowing to the world, heralds a return to the growing season as her myth implies. She ventures into the underworld to rescue her daughter, Persephone, bringing springtime growth and fertility back to the land.

Demeter is especially sensitive to those who are experiencing suffering and grief, and she will assuage these afflictions when called upon to do so. She is one of the triple goddesses, sharing the triad with Persephone (the Maiden) and Hecate (the Crone).

As I'm writing this, it's springtime, and appropriately I'm getting ready to plant my annuals – herbs, and vegetables, and those stalwart staples such as petunias and pansies and marigolds. If you're planning a garden, or if you'd like to add some magic to your garden in the form of herbs and greenery, here's a list of three plants that I'm going to be purchasing in the coming week:

Lavender
Gender: Masculine (or projective)
Planet: Mercury
Element: Air
Magickal Energies: Love, sleep, romance, purification, distressing, communication, enhancement of creative energy

I most often use lavender in mojo bags and poppets aimed at romance; for mojo bags kept beneath pillows to enhance sleep; for candle spells to remove negative and stressful energies from an individual, from a set of circumstances, or from a particular space. Burn a yellow candle dressed in Witch's Oil and rolled in crushed lavender before beginning a project connected with communication, such as a writing project or assignment, or a personal letter. Keep a bowl of lavender by the computer for this same magickal enhancement, because this is an area that is engulfed in the energy and act of communicating with others. Finally, at the end of the day, drop a sprig or two in your bathwater to de-stress, to find peace and comfort, to shed the energies of all those people with whom you've come in contact all day long.

Rosemary
Gender: Masculine (or projective)
Planet: Sun
Element: Fire
Magickal Energies: Protection, cleansing, purification, exorcism, healing, beauty/youth

I use rosemary for cleansing a space of unwanted negative energy. You can add it to the water you're going to use to scrub the floor; burn it, using the smoke to magickally smudge an area; hang dried bunches of the plant in the four corners of a room, over the threshold of doorways, or above the windows. I've made a tincture of rosemary to use as an astringent for my face: I took a nice size bottle, filled it with spring water, added a pretty sprig of rosemary and let it sit and steep overnight, in the moonlight. The next day you can remove the sprig of rosemary, though I chose to leave mine in the bottle, and refrigerate. To apply it, just pour a little on a cotton-ball and use it to wipe down your face *after* you've washed your face as usual to remove makeup. Not only is the rosemary good for your complexion, you are tapping into the magickal energy of this herb to preserve the appearance of youth and beauty.

Embracing the Goddess

In the throes of suffering, when your world is at its bleakest, remember that there is a divine presence who can help you weather this difficult period in your life. Call upon this goddess to sustain you, to support you, to carry you when you're too worn out by life to walk the path.

Demeter is the patron goddess of my garden, bringing her energy of fertility and agricultural growth and abundance to my sacred outdoor spaces. Leave an offering of grain or fruit for the wild things, knowing that this goddess will be drawn to this offering and your space as well.

Demeter's Correspondences

Herbs: Grains/oats, barley, wheat
Animal: Burrowing animals that awaken with spring
Color: Green
Planet: Earth (Gaia)
Day: All seven
Element: Earth
Feminine Face: Mother
Symbol: Cornucopia filled with fruits and grain

Eostre

Her Story
Eostre, sometimes called Ostara, is a Saxon/Germanic goddess of spring. "Eostre" is an ancient word meaning "spring". This goddess celebrates the spring equinox, the beginning of this season, and a return of fertility to the world. The Christians hijacked Eostre's festival to celebrate the resurrection of their Christ, along with her symbols of rejuvenation and fertility: the hare and the egg.

It's interesting to note that the date of the Christian holiday of Easter moves every year. It always falls on the *first* Sunday after the *first* full moon after the spring equinox. There is no escaping our pagan roots.

Just as Christ and Buddha and Mohammed, and all the other gurus of enlightenment and spirituality, grasp the hand of their initiates and lead them onto the path of their philosophy, so too does the goddess Eostre. She will lead you to the threshold of rejuvenation, allowing perhaps one backward glance to see where you've come from so you will appreciate where you're going to. She will forge new cobbled roads of life, with plenty of sights to see and interesting places to stop. She will cast a fertile shadow on your ambitions, allowing you to achieve more than you dreamed possible.

Eostre is galvanizing positive energy. She is birth (spring) after you've experienced death (winter). She is the epitome of what all human beings need to sustain themselves.

Eostre is hope.

Embracing the Goddess
Just as spring returns to the earth out of the depths of winter, along with light and fertility, so too can we rise from the depths

of despair and the dark places to enter the world of light and promise. Call upon Eostre when you need assistance leaving darkness and adversity behind; she'll gladly take you by the hand and lead you into the light.

Eostre's Correspondences

Herbs: Springtime flowers, flowers with yellow, pink, and blue blossoms

Animal: Hare

Color: Yellow, pink, blue

Planet: Earth

Day: All seven

Element: Earth

Feminine Face: Maiden

Symbol: Decorated eggs

Flora

Her Story

Flora, the Roman goddess of spring, rules flowers, foliage, and springtime. Her festivals are celebrated in April and early May. Flora's energies and influences include the protection of vegetation from disease, flowering plants and fruits, as well as menstruation – the flowering of young girls into budding womanhood.

The Blood of the Moon (menstrual blood) is one of the most powerful magickal potions known. Menstrual blood is used in a variety of spells for love, as well as hexing, and has been used traditionally as such since ancient times. It is strongly connected to Flora through her very essence as a goddess of maturation, flowering, coming of age, the ascension to womanhood.

In biblical times, menstruating women were considered unclean and banished to the Red Tent. Here they sat out their isolation from the rest of the community until their period stopped and they had completed a rigorous "cleansing" ritual. Only after that were they allowed to resume normal life among the general population.

Unclean? Really? I don't think so.

I have a different theory for their reasons behind isolating menstruating women: *they were afraid of them.*

In those very ancient times, still immersed closely in pagan roots and practices, the power of menstrual blood and a menstruating woman would have been very clear in their minds, very close to their hearts. The people of this time were caught in a struggle, a struggle between the old ways, the old religion – Goddess worship, natural earth-based spirituality – and the new religions of Judaism and Christianity. The true power of women would have still been common knowledge.

Embrace this aspect of your womanhood. Understand the inspiration behind menstruation of creation and magick, strength, mystery, and miracles. Align your energies with the Blood of the Moon. Celebrate the miracle you are.

Embracing the Goddess

Flora's most amazing magic, aside from a landscape full of beautiful blossoms, is the budding of young girls into maturity, the coming of age that brings with it the menstrual cycle, emphasizing the feminine connection to the moon and its power, fertility, and passage into womanhood.

Western civilization seems to keep the blossoming of female puberty shrouded in out-dated shame and secrecy. When a girl gets her first period, it's generally not something that is mentioned, much less celebrated, particularly in mixed company. By contrast, in the Apache Native American tradition, the onset of menstruation is a time of open celebration for the entire community. There are days of rigorous rituals involving a tribal celebration of young girls who are coming of age. They celebrate the fertility insinuated by the beginning of menstruation. They celebrate pride in feminine puberty and growth. They celebrate the wonder of nature and the miracle that it truly is.

Call upon Flora to celebrate the coming of age for yourself, your daughter, your granddaughter, your nieces, or other young women in your life. Emphasize how special this time is, how beautiful, and how fulfilling it will be.

Flora's Correspondences

Herbs: Mugwort, oleander, tulip, barley, primrose
Animal: Dove
Color: Green, brown
Planet: Gaia (earth)
Day: All seven
Element: Earth

Feminine Face: Maiden
Symbol: Spring flowers

Freya

Her Story

Freya is the Norse goddess of love and war, "Queen of the Valkyries" and "Mistress of Cats", a divine escort for the souls of the dead and especially for fallen warriors, taking them through to the afterlife.

This goddess is considered a poets' muse and inspiration. She's invoked for issues involving relationships, particularly in matters of love and family. Freya is also a potent goddess in matters of sensuality and sexuality, igniting passion. She is considered the most beautiful of the goddesses and totally irresistible to mortal males.

In honor of Freya, Mistress of the Cats, here's a wee bit of herbal cat magick. Use the correspondences for this goddess, as well as the correspondences for this herb, to cast some wild, wicked cat magick.

Catnip is commonly used in sleeping potions. The easiest and most pleasant way I can think of to use catnip for this purpose is to make a delicious pot of tea. Catnip is one of the herbs that I grow in my own garden, so all I have to do when I want to brew a pot of catnip tea is to step outside and snatch a handful of the fresh herb. I usually use both the flowers and the leaves. How much you use is going to depend upon how strong you like your tea and the size of your pot. You can sweeten it with honey or sugar. Since catnip is a member of the mint family, I'm guessing that if you like mint in your tea, you'll like catnip, though to me it is more pungent.

Catnip has an absolutely intoxicating effect on cats, and it was actually hard getting the catnip started in my garden because my cats wouldn't leave it alone. I'd plant a nice lush bunch of catnip, and the next morning I'd go out to find nothing but bare stems. I can't tell you how many times we've looked out the kitchen windows to watch one of our cats, or a stray cat, rolling around our garden in drunken bliss.

Catnip is sacred to all pagan gods/goddesses who manifest as a cat or feline creature, including Sekhmet, Bast, Mau, Tefnut, Mafdet, and Freya.

Correspondences for Catnip

Energy: Feminine (Receptive)
Planet: Venus
Element: Water
Magick: Cat magick, love, beauty, wellbeing

It's believed that a gift of catnip from you to your cat will create a magickal and psychic bond between the two of you. Since I've experienced this myself, I have to say that it truly works in beautiful ways. If you make a catnip talisman for your kitty, keep this in mind. Remember that concentrating on your intentions when crafting magickal items imbues that object with the magick.

Catnip is also used in love spells, often as an ingredient in mojo bags or candle magick. Just as the cat finds this herb intoxicating and irresistible, so will the one you target in love magick, using catnip to draw them to you. Hang a bunch of dried catnip over the threshold of your home to draw good spirits and good luck, as well as to draw the blessings of cat goddesses. Catnip is also used in beauty spells, either as a tincture you can use to bathe your face, or with candle magic. It's believed that this herb will mesmerize those targeted in such spells to see you as youthful and beautiful. This type of enchantment is considered a glamoury.

Embracing the Goddess

Freya is the goddess for all of us "Crazy Cat Ladies", and I'm proud to count myself in this company. Call upon this goddess when working cat magic, to call upon the cat as a totem animal, or just to honor this magical creature.

Freya's Correspondences

Herbs: Catnip, geranium, willow, goldenrod, magnolia
Animal: Cat
Color: Green, pink
Planet: Venus
Day: Friday
Element: Water
Feminine Face: Maiden
Symbol: Cats, the number 13

Green Tara

Her Story

Green Tara is known as "The Mother of Compassion". She's worshipped in a variety of Hindu and Buddhist traditions and guards against natural disasters; the elements of Mother Nature. Green Tara nurtures humanity on a worldly level, alleviating suffering and misery. This goddess influences self-mastery through meditation and can be called upon to help us strengthen those areas of our personality, ego, and self-esteem which need improvement.

Light a green candle to Green Tara and recite the mantra below out loud, over and over again if necessary, until you believe it with all your heart:

If I am weak, I will be strong; if I am stubborn, I will be flexible; if I am arrogant, I will be humble; if I am cruel, I will be kind.

I will succeed at all endeavors, and if I should slip up on one or two, it won't be because I have not tried. I am intelligent and worthy of success. I am beautiful inside and out; I am creative; I am sensitive; I am healthy; I am cunning; I am energetic; I am a shaker and a mover; I am a good wife, mother, daughter... I am an exceptional wife; I am an exceptional mother; I am an exceptional daughter.

I shine.

I succeed.

I am.

Embracing the Goddess

When going through any type of life crisis, whether physical illness, mental challenges, or self-esteem issues, Green Tara can be invoked for deep meditation, allowing us to safely journey within ourselves to find and follow the paths least trod within our psyche. She will open new doors of understanding, enabling us to grow from within and manifest our growth to the physical world around us.

Green Tara's Correspondences

Herbs: Eyebright, marjoram, mint, slippery elm, anise
Animal: Sow, raven, mare, owl
Color: Green, yellow
Planet: Mercury
Day: Wednesday
Element: Air
Feminine Face: Maiden
Symbol: Malachite, emerald, mirrors (for self-examination)

Hathor

Her Story

Hathor is the Egyptian goddess of love and beauty, wealth, music, and the arts. She rules womanhood and femininity and is the patron goddess of dancers and musicians. Worship Hathor with offerings of rich perfumes, songs, and dance rituals. This goddess is most often depicted as a beautiful woman with the ears of a cow and carrying a sistrum.

The Skrying Mirror

There is an ancient Egyptian tradition steeped in the mystery of the skrying mirror and the goddess Hathor. It's said that if you create a skrying mirror consecrated to this goddess, the mirror will give you the power of vision that enables you to see your strengths and your weaknesses when you gaze into it. This is, in itself, an amazing revelation if you are strong enough and honest enough with yourself to accept what you see without flinching.

The skrying mirror is actually an old divinatory practice. Not only will you see your strengths and your weaknesses, which will allow you to adjust your energy and retain your personal power, but you will also be blessed with a second sight that allows you to see visions of prophecy and revelation. It allows you to view the past and glean information from it, and it allows you to look into the future, giving you the ability to direct your destiny.

A skrying mirror is not a piece of reflective glass, but a black surface. You can easily transform a traditional mirror into a skrying mirror by painting the surface. The important part will be consecrating it to the goddess Hathor with candles and herbs, incense and music.

Embracing the Goddess

Embrace Hathor by celebrating your womanhood and the passage of its stages, from maiden, to mother, to crone, with rituals, music, and dance. Know that you are beautiful in all phases of life, in all sizes and shapes.

Know this and accept it.

Hathor's Correspondences

Herbs: Myrrh, goldenrod, lavender, cardamom, hibiscus
Animal: Cow
Color: Yellow, pink, green
Planet: Mercury, Venus
Day: Wednesday, Friday
Element: Air, Water
Feminine Face: Mother
Symbol: Sistrum, mirror

Hecate

Her Story

Hecate is one of the triple goddesses, often depicted in art as a single body with three heads. She is the goddess of witchcraft; the moon; the spirit realm; nature and night visions; considered protectress of the witches. She also protects women in childbirth, is the guardian of the spirit world, and "Queen of the Crossroads" – a place of dark magic, spiritual wisdom, and terrible power.

The moon's shadow fell as a pattern on the dirt road beneath the trees. The young woman's cloak hid her face as she leaned on her knees to dig a small hole, depositing a knotted scarf holding herbs and stones, a tiny carved image, and her menstrual blood. Her lips moved silently as she invoked the presence of Hecate.

As the young woman covered her sacred bundle with earth and rose from her knees, the sound of a hound baying at the moon echoed in the distance. The breeze picked up, moving the tree limbs above, shifting the shadows on the road into eerie patterns. A chill ran up the woman's spine, and she gathered her cloak more tightly about her shoulders, shivering with the knowledge that the great goddess Hecate was moving through the crossroads.

Embracing the Goddess

Don't be afraid to stand up for yourself. So often women are under the impression that someone else is responsible for their protection, but this isn't true. We're responsible for protecting ourselves, and sometimes this can mean making difficult decisions.

Hecate's Correspondences

Herbs: Garlic, lavender, honey
Animal: Dog
Color: Purple
Planet: Jupiter
Day: Thursday
Element: Earth
Feminine Face: Crone
Symbols: Torch, dagger, crossroads, the moon, serpent, fire

Invoke this goddess in the sacred darkness of night, at a crossroads, which is her favored realm, in the light of a fire. The presence of a dog is desirable, and this creature will not only be pleasing to Hecate, but may very well announce her beautiful and terrible presence before you are aware of it.

Inanna

Her Story

Inanna is an ancient Sumerian goddess of love and war; known as Ishtar to the Babylonians, she was worshiped as the "Queen of Heaven and Hell" in Mesopotamia. She is a lunar goddess, believed to be embodied in the morning and evening stars. Inanna influences fertility and was invoked for ancient mating rituals. As a warrior goddess, she protects city dwellers from invaders, dispenses justice, and imparts the wisdom of life and death.

From within all women, the seed will grow:
the seeds of life
the seeds of creativity
the seeds of joy
the seeds of wisdom
the seeds of ambition
the seeds of independence
the seeds of success
the seeds of love
the seeds of life
the seeds of continuity
the seeds of ancestry
the seeds of the future

Embracing the Goddess

Women suffering the pain of infertility can turn to the goddess Inanna for renewal and inspiration. Inanna will hear your call and grant you the miracle of conception, the wisdom for this undertaking, and the strength to carry it through.

Inanna's Correspondences

Herbs: Frankincense, nutmeg, wormwood, sunflower, hyssop

Animal: Lion

Color: Orange, red

Planet: Mars

Day: Tuesday

Element: Fire

Feminine Face: Maiden

Symbol: Eight-point star

Isis

Her Story

Isis is the Egyptian goddess of healing and magic. She epitomizes the ideal of wife and mother, and is the patroness of women and children, marriage and marriage vows. Her energies affect or assist transformations, ancestral bonds, and manifestation of changes. Isis is perhaps one of the best known Egyptian deities and is famous for her loyalty to her spouse, searching the four corners of Egypt in order to retrieve, reconstruct, and resurrect her murdered and mutilated husband Osiris.

Sometimes we expect an awful lot from our spouses. Sometimes we expect them to live up to ideal of the fairytale knight-in-shining-armor. Sometimes we expect them to be all that we ever imagined. Sometimes we expect them to satisfy our every wish (without telling them what it is). Sometimes we expect them to be bigger-than-life. Sometimes we expect them to be perfect.
Sometimes we expect too much.

- Why do you love your spouse?
- What drew you to this person in the first place?
- What do you have in common?
- What are all the opposites about the two of you?
- If you could change one thing about your spouse, what would it be?
- If your spouse could change one thing about you, what would it be?
- Is there a "Deal Breaker" in this relationship; if so, what is it?
- Do you trust your spouse?
- Does your spouse trust you?
- Does jealousy rear its ugly head?

- Do you respect each other?
- Do you always tell each other the truth?
- In life's worst-case-scenario, could you depend on your spouse?

If this person were to die tomorrow...

- What would you regret not saying to them?
- What would you regret not doing with them?
- How would their absence impact your life?

Embracing the Goddess

Call upon Isis when matters of family are on the line, when protection is needed, when loyalties come into play, when bonds need strengthening or protecting from destructive outside influences. Carry a talisman of this goddess on your wedding day to manifest and magnify the unbreakable bond of love, marriage vows, and life-long commitment.

Isis's Correspondences

Herbs: Lotus flower, cypress tree
Animal: Eagle,
Color: Pink, green, turquoise
Planet: Venus
Day: Friday
Element: Water
Feminine Face: Mother
Symbol: Tyet (Knot of Isis), eagle wings

Kali Ma

Her Story

Kali Ma embraces the wild and untamed spirit of womanhood. She is the warrior goddess who can fight her battles with the vengeful lust of a soldier. She is the goddess of time, ruling both chaos and order, for out of one comes the other. Kali Ma is most often depicted as a coal black image dressed in human remains, wearing a necklace of skulls. It is her wrath, her unabashed terrible energy, that you call upon when you need protection. Scream her name with all the fervor of a demon goddess, and she will come to your aid.

The female voice rose in a howl of anger and defiance, *"Kali Ma!!!"*

Before the man's fist could touch this woman's face a second time, there was a deep rumbling in the sky, as though a storm were brewing, ready to unleash. Something about the sound caused the man to pause in mid-swing, his fist only inches from his victim's cheekbone. A look of utter horror crawled across his face; he glanced only for a second into the woman's eyes and understood what he saw there. He was afraid, very afraid, and he turned and ran, the deep rumbling sound of thunder chasing him down the alley in ruthless pursuit.

Embracing the Goddess

There are times in life when women have to figuratively take up the club, the sword, the bow, and stand their ground to fight; fighting for their rights, their families, and sometimes even their life. Don't hesitate to embrace the warrior goddess within you, call upon her strength and her furious power whenever you need it. Rejoice in this wild woman.

Kali Ma's Correspondences

Herbs: Hellebore, morning glory, skullcap

Color: Black

Planet: Saturn

Day: Saturday

Element: All four

Feminine Face: Crone

Symbols: Skull, bones

Kuan Yin

Her Story

Kuan Yin is a Chinese goddess of mercy, but has become so popular she transcends cultural and religious boundaries. She is a caretaker for deceased souls, comforting them, guiding them through the etheric realm to their next destination. She is the goddess of healing, curing ailments of the body, mind, and soul. This goddess is also a protectress and can be called upon to protect especially women, children, and animals. She also protects the traveler, whether by land, or air, or sea. Kuan Yin breaks the cycle of rebirth, retribution, and punishment.

Kuan Yin, Mother Goddess, I do not know what to do.
I invoke Thee, in thy infinite wisdom and mercy, to open your arms to your daughter.
Speak to me, Mother.
Direct me towards the path I should follow, gently lead me down the road I am to travel.
And during this journey,
May I feel your hand upon my shoulder,
May I hear your whisper in my ear.
May I feel your love in my heart.

Embracing the Goddess

Kuan Yin is the Asian version of the Virgin Mary, showing compassion on the multitudes, on the earth, and on the creatures that dwell upon it. Invoke this goddess when you need help, when you need confirmation, when you need a divinity who will have your back and support you in times of crisis. Call upon this goddess for the purity and regeneration of her energy.

Kuan Yin's Correspondences

Herbs: Oleander, tulip, knotweed, primrose, honeysuckle, orange
   blossoms, lotus

Animal: Horses, peacock

Color: White, green, brown

Planet: Earth

Day: All seven

Element: Earth

Feminine Face: Mother

Symbols: Rosary, lotus blossom, sutra vase, willow branch

Lakshmi

Her Story

Lakshmi is the Hindu goddess of prosperity, her name implies "Good Luck". She embraces the epitome of wealth and abundance in the material world as well as in the spiritual realm, and she is a household goddess favored by women. October is the month that is traditionally set aside to celebrate Lakshmi, and full moons are sacred to her, embracing the feminine face of the Mother.

This goddess is depicted as a beautiful woman with a golden complexion, usually seated on an open lotus blossom holding a lotus bud, which represents beauty, fertility, and purity. Lakshmi has four hands which represent four aspects of life: dharma (righteousness); karma (desires); artha (wealth); and moksha (liberation from the cycle of death and rebirth).

It's a warm rainy summer day as I write this, and I'm in the midst of revamping a downstairs room that has been left vacant with the departure of a child now grown up. I stand in the center of this space, still able to feel the personality of the individual who occupied it for so many years. This leaves me with a feeling of wistfulness and nostalgia, but also with an understanding of the progression of time and the life changes that must come to us all.

I'm going to call upon the goddess Lakshmi to bless this space, to clear it in preparation for its new occupant, and to bless the activities that will ensue within its four walls.

May peace reside within this room.
May wisdom visit with each full moon.

May the spirits of my sisters past,
Hold tight the memories,
That they might last,

For future generations of women true,
Pass this wisdom, this mystery, this glory to.

So mote it be.

Embracing the Goddess

Housewives, call upon Lakshmi to bless and consecrate the sacred space that is your home. Allow her energy to fill the space and to inspire you. Whether you live in the most fantastic of mansions, or the humblest abode, remember that you have the ability to turn this space into something beautiful, something peaceful, something inspiring and inviting. As you work to create a beautiful physical atmosphere in which to live, you may find that you are creating the same thing on a spiritual level as well.

Lakshmi's Correspondences

Herbs: Mugwort, oleander, anise,
Animal: Spider
Color: Red and gold (traditional colors), purple
Planet: Jupiter
Day: Thursday
Element: Earth
Feminine Face: Mother
Symbols: Lotus blossom, gold coins

Lilith

Her Story

Lilith is considered the original "Queen of Heaven", and in her glory days she was known as Adam's first wife, a dirty little secret that's been hard to sweep under the proverbial rug. Lilith is known for her dominating nature, her unquenchable lust, and her appetite for newborn infants. She raises storms and tempests with fiery might, sucks the life-juice out of men as they sleep, and prowls the night in search of unprotected infants to satisfy her hunger.

In spite of the harsh side to this complicated goddess, you can invoke Lilith when this is the very energy that is needed, just don't invoke Lilith in a home where there is a young child. And beware, her energy is powerful and unforgiving.

The woman writhed uncontrollably in the flickering light from the hearth, clenching the rough hand-woven blanket between her teeth. The pain passed, and her body relaxed. But the next pain would come, and the next, and the next... until there would be a child. The old wise-woman seeing to this village birth rose stiffly to place another piece of wood on the fire. She went then, to the laboring mother's cot, and gently slid her hand beneath the down-filled pillow, her fingers searching for the protective iron talisman. She breathed a sigh of relief when her fingertips touched the cold metal.

A noise on the roof of the thatched hut caused both the mother and the midwife to turn their faces upward in fear and foreboding. But there was silence, only silence and a soft wind rustling around the corners of the cottage.

The demon goddess Lilith would not enter this cottage on this night. Lilith would not claim this child, not this child, not tonight.

Embracing the Goddess

Lilith is all about lust and quenching appetites that are not considered genteel in the more prudish circles of society. But the pagan woman knows that when such energy is needed, when it's desired, and when it can be used to her advantage, she can invoke this goddess with the promise of fulfillment in these areas. The pagan woman will also know how to protect herself from the harsher side of this demon goddess.

Lilith's Correspondences

Herbs: Sage, marjoram, slippery elm

Animal: Screech owl

Color: Yellow

Planet: Mercury

Day: Wednesday

Element: Air

Feminine Face: Maiden

Symbol: Dark moon

Metal: Iron (Lilith detests this metal and it is often used in amulets and protective spells against her.)

Lucina

Her Story

Lucina is a Roman goddess of light. She is the protectress of women in child-birth and the newborn infant. It is Lucina who guides new life into the world. In ancient times, at the height of worship to this goddess, Roman women and girls would do knot magick to call upon the power of Lucina to protect the birthing mother and newborn child. They would untie knots previously created in long lengths of material, and they would unplait their braided hair, all to prevent unpleasant entanglements during the birth process.

Knot Magick

In most traditions knot magick is employed with the use of a 9 foot long red cord or ribbon. But I find that knot magick is so very versatile that I use different colored ribbons, depending upon the magickal intention: *green,* for health and healing, or prosperity; *red,* for passion, love, lust, and romance, but also, as in this case, for childbirth; *yellow,* for mental endeavors and creative projects, as well as for communication; *purple,* for legal and business issues, but also for calling in spirits; *blue,* for psychism and dreams, for divination, and for those ethereal realms of mermaids, fairies and dragons, and other creatures of myth and legend.

We're going to work this magick under the guidance of the goddess Lucina, and we're going to work this magick for the safe delivery of a healthy baby into this world. Whether we're working this magick for ourselves (Yes, it's okay to take care of yourself!), or for our daughters, nieces, sisters, mothers, aunts, or friends, you can do this.

You have the power to invoke this goddess in this magick and have your hand, figuratively, on this child's head, as a blessing.

(Cast this magick *before* the full moon that comes *before* the due date, and then keep this knotted ribbon in a safe place until the time to release it. Begin undoing these knots and releasing all this wonderful positive energy *at the time that labor begins*.)

First, set the stage, so to speak, create the sacred space to invoke and welcome Lucina. You'll want a tall white pillar candle for the center piece (the goddess candle); and you'll want to circle this with several red votive candles (nine would be nice). The incense could be myrrh, but you can use a scent that resonates with you; my favorite is nag champa. You can be as ritualistic as you care to be. If you love music and dance, you can invoke Lucina in a blaze of glory. But if this type of thing isn't your cup of tea, you will be just as successful at invoking this energy by simply lighting your candles and incense before you begin.

Nine knots you're going to tie, drawing in your intention with each one, reciting a mantra over and over. Don't be alarmed if this mantra, this chanting, turns into a frenzied, almost incoherent whisper. This simply means that you're entering an alpha state, where energy is being moved and magick is possible.

Chant your chant, tie your knots, lose yourself in this experience.

When you're finished, extinguish the flame on the white goddess candle, but leave the red votive candles to burn themselves out.

Place this red knotted ribbon in a safe place, and begin the vigil, the age-old vigil of waiting for that first pain, that first glorious sign of impending birth. It's then that you will bring this ribbon out and begin undoing the knots, feeling the joy and the happy anticipation.

Embracing the Goddess

Of course, the power and magick of this goddess will be called upon for laboring women and their infants. Call upon this goddess in happy anticipation of a complication free delivery.

Gather mothers, aunts, sisters, female friends and cousins to the laboring woman's side to ritually unknot their braided hair, or long strips of red linen that were previously knotted in happy anticipation of this event (perhaps at the baby shower!).

Lucina's Correspondences

Herbs: Moonwort, peach, lemon balm, willow, myrrh

Color: White, silver, blue, red (feminine blood)

Planet: Moon

Day: Monday

Element: Water

Feminine Face: Mother

Symbol: The knot, blood, full moon

Mama Cocha

Her Story

Mama Cocha is an Incan sea goddess, called "Mother of the Ocean". Her prime attributes are protecting fisherman and sailors, and those who make their living from the sea.

At the time of this writing, I've never seen the ocean. One of my daughters traveled to the west coast this summer and saw the ocean for the first time. I listened to her wide-eyed rapt descriptions with bated breath.

"You can smell the ocean a long time before you see it," she began. She went on, trying to tell me what it smells like, what it looks like, what it sounds like, what it feels like. She also brought me back a bottle filled with sand from the beach she stood upon. It is a precious thing.

I realize that her experience, what she felt, was both universal and unique to her, and that when I get to see the ocean for the first time, what I feel will be unique to me, yet there will be something universal about it as well.

The ocean is considered the place where all life began. No wonder the goddesses who are connected with the ocean are considered powerful and are revered, filled with the energy of the creatrix. It is the epitome of the Goddess, the ocean. As a familiar ritual song implies: we're but a single drop of rain, and after our lives have been lived and run their course, we will return to the arms of our mother. We will merge into the ocean of spirits and soar in universal knowledge and universal love.

Embracing the Goddess

The oceans cover more than 90% of Earth, and just as Gaia is enveloped within the blue mists and veils of water, so you can be enveloped within this mother's embrace by calling upon this goddess for protection. I've discovered that Mama Cocha, famous for protecting those who travel on water, also offers her protection to those who live beyond the sea, through the power of the element of Water.

Mama Cocha's Correspondences

Herbs: Seaweed, water lily, club moss, calamus
Animal: Dolphin
Color: Blue, white, aqua
Planet: Moon
Day: Monday, Tuesday
Element: Water
Feminine Face: Mother
Symbol: Mermaid

Mami Wata

Her Story

Mami Wata is another African water goddess. She embraces the symbols that are so universal to the Mother Goddess, those symbols that encompass so many cultures from all over the world. Offer Mami Wata rich perfumes and sweet liquids to satisfy her cravings so she will bestow upon you prosperity, good health, and healing. Make offerings to Mami Wata at bedtime so that she will enrich your dreams with visions.

I see pictures in my mind sent to me by the universe. I see pictures in my dreams. I see pictures in my waking moments, overlaid across real life before my physical eyes. As voices around me speak, people moving through normal life, the sounds take on patterns, and colors, and movement connected to objects in this, the earth plane... and it all comes together to form a collage, a beautiful miraculous pattern of life.

Embracing the Goddess

Use the energy of Mami Wata with the element of Water for magick and inspiration through dreams and visions, divinatory practices, and the strengthening of your personal intuition.

Mami Wata's Correspondences

Herbs: African violet, comfrey, eucalyptus, moonwort, kava-kava
Animal: Dolphin
Color: Blue, white, silver
Planet: Moon
Day: Monday
Element: Water
Feminine Face: Maiden
Symbol: Mermaid

Morrigan

Her Story

Morrigan is the Irish goddess of prophecy, a warrior goddess, often portrayed as a brunette beauty of great strength and cunning. She is connected to the battlefield and is known as "The Witch Queen of Death". She helps fallen soldiers pass to the other side. This Celtic sorceress rules the powers of prediction and enchantment, and the more squalid, volatile aspects of love and sex.

As I write this, the world and the news coverage is awash with the grizzly execution of an American journalist abroad. As I'm reading the paragraph above, about Morrigan and how she helps fallen soldiers, I'm hoping that it was She who was there to help this hero cross over.

For every civilian who valiantly gives their life for a righteous and worthy cause, for every soldier who falls in battle fighting for truth and freedom, may the great Goddess Morrigan take them by the hand and lead them through the wreckage of civilization to the glorious peace of the Summerland.
So mote it be.

Embracing the Goddess

Invoke the energy of Morrigan to protect your loved one in battle; for all soldiers overseas, that they may be kept safe; and that they may have her support and guidance should they fall in battle. Invoke the energy of this goddess if you find yourself in a volatile and unstable romantic relationship. She will lend her warrior energy for self-protection, and she will guide you through the maze to a clear horizon.

Morrigan's Correspondences

Herbs: Cinnamon, cayenne pepper, ginger, dragon's blood, witch hazel

Animal: Battle horse

Color: Orange, red

Planet: Mars

Day: Tuesday

Element: Fire

Feminine Face: Mother

Symbols: Battleshield, sword

Oshun

Her Story

Oshun is an Yoruban goddess celebrated in West Africa as a patroness of women and witches. She can also be found in some traditions of Santeria. She rules all bodies of water and all acts of sensuality. Oshun is the hedonistic nature within all women; she rolls in unabashed lust and physical delight with nary a qualm of guilt. Make offerings to this goddess of jewelry, tantalizing perfumes, and sea shells.

Oshun is most often depicted as a female with large hips, and she is a triple goddess in the triad with Oba and Oya.

Who are all the lovers in your life? How has each one touched your life, whether good or bad or indifferent, whether climactic or anti-climactic? What did you learn from them?

Everyone comes into our life, whether permanently or just for a season, for a reason. Not all relationships are meant to last forever. And when a couple decides to end a relationship, it does not mean failure. It does not necessarily mean that someone did something wrong; it does not necessarily mean there is a "good guy" and a "bad guy" in this situation. It simply means that the relationship has run its course, and it's time for both parties to move on with their lives.

I've run into people within our society who were brought up under strict Christian (and Catholic) homes and divorce was frowned upon, or even forbidden. I had a heated head to head argument with one lady (Southern Baptist) about this very topic. She believed that once you were married, you were married forever – *No Matter What.*

No matter what? What if you were abused? What if you were incompatible? What if you were unhappy? People change over time; needs change; personalities change; goals change; spirituality changes; physical needs and desires change; hopes and fears change. Life is not static.

I believe that most human beings, living an average human lifespan, will have not just one, but many lovers during their life time. As they should.

Let go of the guilt.

It's all good.

Embracing the Goddess

Women coming from patriarchal-based spiritual backgrounds often have a difficult time letting go of unnecessary guilt; guilt for a variety of reasons, but most often encompassing their sexuality and sensuality. If this is your issue, call upon the goddess Oshun to open you up to your true nature. Invoke this goddess to celebrate your sexuality, to wallow in unadulterated physical pleasure. Invoke this goddess and let her re-introduce you to healthy womanhood.

Oshun's Correspondences

Herbs: Belladonna, cardamom, raspberry, foxglove, hibiscus, strawberry

Color: Blue

Planet: Moon

Day: Monday

Element: Water

Feminine Face: Mother

Symbols: Sea shells, undines

Pele

Her Story

Pele is the famous volcano goddess of Hawaii. She is depicted as a beautiful sensuous woman; and she is noted for being an alluring seductress, seducing males ruthlessly and relentlessly. Pele is also known for her volatile temper, a bitch among the goddesses, and it's been said that many an unsuspecting tourist has brought down her wrath by removing a volcanic stone from her mountainside.

It's okay to be a bitch. Our society, mainstream mostly Christian society, has beaten it into little girls' heads that we must always be "nice", always, with no exceptions. Pele teaches us otherwise, telling us it's okay to get up on our back legs and howl and screech when we feel the need; it's okay to use our feminine wiles of seduction; it's okay to pull no stops, to use our femininity to our advantage. Society – watch out, Pele has turned us loose.

Embracing the Goddess

Invoke Pele with the element of Fire to turn your inner Wild Woman loose. When it's time to abandon "nice", invoke Pele for the passion and fury needed to stand your ground, make your point, fight your battle, confront your adversary, or seduce your target.

Pele's Correspondences

Herbs: Angelica, mandrake, tobacco, wormwood, rowan, bloodroot
Color: Red, orange
Planet: Mars
Day: Tuesday
Element: Fire
Feminine Face: Mother
Symbols: Fire, lava rock

Persephone

Her Story

Persephone is the Greek goddess of spring. She rules agriculture, growth, and new opportunities; she epitomizes the natural magic of spring and the sprouting of new vegetation after the dark of winter. Known as "Queen of the Underworld", this goddess is the "Keeper of Souls". She also ruthlessly carries through the curses of men upon the souls of the dead. Persephone influences the wisdom of life and death, magick and divination.

Persephone is the daughter of Zeus and Demeter, a harvest goddess, and is most known for her abduction by Hades into the underworld. It's when her mother Demeter comes to find and rescue her, returning Persephone to the world, that spring returns.

For the goddess skilled in divination, through the tarot, what wisdom has she for us?

3 of Swords (Reversed)... The Fool... Ace of Wands (Reversed)
2 of Pentacles... 3 of Pentacles
7 of Swords (Reversed)

Through a series of heartaches and disappointments, we find ourselves on a new path, one of several in our life-time perhaps. New beginnings are right around the corner; but each beginning, we must realize, stems from an ending. Remember not to drag debris from life's earlier disappointments throughout your entire journey.

In all things there will be balance; the universe and the higher powers will see to that. Work will be our salvation; it will be our strength, and it will be the solution to many of the issues from this life and past lives. We'll find strength, power, self-confidence, happiness, and a sense of fulfillment in the work we do, the contribution we make.

Along this journey, you may run into people who feel they can take advantage of you, of your success, of your energy. Do not worry here, for what they think they are stealing is nothing of importance. These are people who do not see the whole picture, people who may have abandoned or turned on you at some point in your life for all the wrong reasons.

Know that you are above the pettiness of the world, you are in fact ready to soar with the Goddess.

Embracing the Goddess

Invoke Persephone to strengthen your second sight and to fine tune your divination skills. Call upon this goddess to bless your garden at the beginning of spring, insuring lush growth and freedom from disease and blight. Use the energy of Persephone to enhance growth, growth regarding material issues, or a flowering of personal endeavors.

Persephone's Correspondences

Herbs: Daisy, ivy, lavender, mint, patchouli
Animal: Bat, parrot, ram
Color: Green, brown
Planet: Earth (Gaia)
Day: All seven
Element: Earth
Feminine Face: Maiden
Symbol: Sheaf of grain, wreath of flowers

Red Tara

Her Story

Red Tara is a Tibetan goddess of transformation. She's worshipped throughout Eurasia in both the Hindu and Buddhist traditions. She manifests transformations at all levels: physical, mental, and spiritual. This goddess highlights positive intentions and actions. She also has the ability to calm wild emotions and turn them into quiet common sense and reasoning. Red Tara is a powerful goddess in that she affects the energies of magick and alchemical processes.

Red Tara, she who rules over physical transformation, manifest for me a healthy body, beautiful in its own unique way.

Red Tara, she who rules over mental transformation, manifest for me a healthy ego, self-confidence, intelligence, and above all, balance.

Red Tara, she who rules over spiritual transformation, manifest for me tranquility and peace, a strong bond with my spiritual path and its practices; and above all, a connection with the Divine that will enlighten me in this lifetime and beyond.

Embracing the Goddess

When you are bat-shit, over-the-hill crazy with anger, collect your wits and invoke Red Tara. She'll calm you down so you can think rationally and react intelligently. "Get a grip!" Red Tara will order you. All magickal practitioners can call upon Red Tara for her energy and transitional qualities when performing magick... yes, casting spells. Her rational calm influence will insure the same in your magick. She'll grab any helter-skelter energy and throttle it, so your magickal endeavors will work correctly.

Red Tara's Correspondences

Herbs: Holly, shallot, basil, cumin, marigold, penny royal, fennel

Color: Red, orange

Planet: Mars

Day: Tuesday

Element: Fire

Feminine Face: Crone

Shakti

Her Story

Shakti is the supreme goddess of India. She's the primal force (female energy) within all other Hindu goddesses, the ancient driving force, the "Breath of Life". Shakti leads women to spiritual enlightenment. She is found in the energy of yoga and many tantric practices.

The Liberated Woman

Who is she?

Is she you?

List three mundane and routine *daily* chores or activities that you do day after day, after day, for yourself, for your family, or for your employer.

List three *daily* practices or activities that you incorporate into your life for your own mental, spiritual, or physical benefit and well-being.

List three people you have positive connections with.

What is your dream?

What are your goals for the next five years?

Who inspires you?

Embracing the Goddess

Connect with Shakti to open or celebrate the crown chakra, to directly connect to the Feminine Divine, to do energy work on a spiritual level. This goddess is an open line to divinity. Invoke her to help you find your way, to answer your questions, to alleviate your doubt. Invoke this goddess to discover who you are, where you came from, and where you're headed.

Shakti's Correspondences

Herbs: Patchouli, mugwort, oleander *(Earth energy)*; dandelion, sage, slippery elm *(Air energy)*; allspice, golden seal, dragon's blood *(Fire energy)*; belladonna, eucalyptus, ragwort *(Water energy)*

Color: Green, brown

Planet: Earth (Gaia)

Day: All seven

Element: Earth

Feminine Face: Mother

Symbols: Kundalini snake, lotus blossom

Shitala

Her Story

Shitala is the Hindu goddess of disease, attributed with the creation of smallpox, among other insidious maladies. Ironically, it is Shitala you call upon to cure illness, to cleanse the body of disease. What a paradox this goddess is! She despises filth and dirt. When invoking Shitala, you must physically cleanse your home or sacred space, and you must have a ritual cleansing bath before beginning. To disregard these actions would mean an unsuccessful invocation.

Healing Candle Spells

For physical maladies, go with the element of Earth, the color green and all the other correspondences that are connected to this element and this type of magick. (You'll find correspondences for the elements, as well as other information to help you craft your magick and cast your spells, at the end of this book.)

But there's so much more to it, and there are so many ways to be ill, or other reasons people need healing.

For mental illness, you will call upon the element of Air, and your candle color will be yellow. For a victim of physical violence, or sexual abuse, you'll use the energies combined of Earth (green for physical healing), Air (yellow for mental healing), and Water (blue for spiritual healing).

For someone who is terminally ill, you will call upon Spirit, and your candle will be white. It will ease their passing and light the path for their journey to the other side. It will invoke their spirit guide, who will take them by the hand, helping them travel safely as they cross over.

Household Blessing

The Tools

White candles; sage, or a cleansing incense like sandalwood, and a bowl or holder for this; bells, if you fancy them; a broom, for symbolism and to "sweep" away negative energy from each room; a bowl of salted water to asperge (sprinkle) each room, *as well as every nook and cranny.*

The Method

I start from the bottom and go up, so begin in the basement, if there is one, or the lowest floor. Basically, you'll go from room to room, cleansing it of negative energy, moving it out and "sweeping" it along until you push it right out of the house with the last room or space you clear.

Enter a room, demand the negative energy and ghosties (or other spirits) leave. Walk clockwise around the room with the salted water first, dipping your fingers in it and sprinkling the space as you go. Then do the same with the incense, smudging the rooms, making sure that you include any closet space or cubbies. Energy lurks in these spaces, you know. That's why children, who are more in tune with it, are often afraid of these little dark closets and corners. For a final flourish, and to make your point to the spirits or other entities trying to take over this space, use the broom to symbolically "sweep" the negative energy right out the door. Sweep from east to west in large whooshes. The broom doesn't even need to touch the floor. After all, you're literally sweeping a space, not the floor itself. Make sure, as you do this, that you are ordering the spirits to leave, that you are reclaiming this space, and that you are in charge. Put some emotion into it!

As a side note, don't be alarmed if you feel a rush of goose bumps up your legs as you're doing this. It's nothing scary, and it's nothing that will harm you. It's just the energy that you're moving; you can often feel it. (Yes, people, it's an actual "Real" thing.)

Embracing the Goddess

Call upon Shitala for the most obvious of reasons: to banish physical illnesses and maladies. Be respectful, be wary, be sure that you appease her with ritual cleansings. Remember that this goddess not only cures illness, she creates it.

Shitala's Correspondences

Herbs: Columbine, lemon balm, myrrh, thyme, lilac
Color: Blue, silver
Planet: Moon
Day: Monday
Element: Water
Feminine Face: Crone

Snake Woman

Her Story

Snake Woman is often considered to be a household and fertility deity, as well as a powerful goddess and priestess. Seduction is her forte. Within the serpent lies her power. She represents the Feminine Mysteries and holds within her realm of magic healing and empowerment throughout all stages of a woman's life. A goddess of Crete, Snake Woman is often depicted bare-breasted, clutching a snake in each hand.

The small group of women, wrapped in brightly colored blankets or clutching a soft shawl about their shoulders to keep off the early morning chill, tread softly on the well-worn path in sandaled feet, rising up through the trees, ever higher onto the hilltop.

At the end of this path, in a small clearing, a flat stone altar has been erected. The centerpiece of this altar is a tall ceramic statue of Snake Woman, her breasts bare to the morning sunrise, two writhing serpents in each of her raised hands. Placed around Snake Woman are a ring of tall red pillar candles rolled in herbs, one candle for each of the women in the group. Within the center of this altar stands a large cast-iron cauldron.

From beneath their blankets and shawls, the women bring forth small scraps of paper with their intentions written upon them... healing for an illness; the strength to make a necessary change; power to transition from mother to crone, from maiden to mother; the desire to find love, to re-ignite the passion of an old love, to celebrate lasting love.

The women stand in a circle around the large flat stone, each woman stepping forward in turn, placing her written intention into the cauldron and then bending to light the red candle before her. When all the candles are lit, the women stand around the circle once more, hand in hand, each one chanting their personal affirmation, their desire, invoking the spirit of Snake Woman. As the chanting rings clear, becoming louder and more intense, one of the women bends to ignite the paper in the cauldron. As the flames rear up, a unified shout rises from the group... and then silence descends.

Embracing the Goddess

If you feel that you've lost the passion in your life for love, passion that drives you to succeed, passion that enables you to wake each day eager to leap into the fray of life, embrace Snake Woman and learn to turn the wild-woman within you loose. Cut the ties that bind with the enthusiasm and energy of this goddess.

Snake Woman's Correspondences

Herbs: Black snakeroot, coriander, goldenseal
Animal: Snake
Colors: Red, orange, yellow
Planet: Sun
Day: Sunday
Element: Fire
Feminine Face: Maiden
Symbols: Snake, wild bare-breasted women

Sophia

Her Story

Sophia is one of the most powerful of goddesses, a goddess of the Middle East, entrenched in the legacy of the Gnostics, of Judeo/Christian culture. She is the ultimate Divine Feminine, the personification of divinity, the ultimate sacred feminine energy and entity of the universe. This goddess takes the patriarchal personification of "God" and stands it on its ear. Sophia is the voice of wisdom from the divine. She is the creatrix of all the universe. It's believed that every human in existence carries a sparkle of her energy within them.

Conversation with the Divine

Universe, I know you're listening. You can be really, really quiet sometimes, trying to trick me into life and stark reality; but I know you're there, and I know you're listening. And I know you can hear me.

Life is running its course... figuratively and literally.

How? How do I know this?

I know this by the living "Flow" of life, in a figurative way, a physical way, an undeniably human/mother nature way.

I know this by moving rushing water in streams, and rivers, and bubbling brooks. I know this by the blood rushing through my veins in a mortal journey between my heart and the rest of my body. I know this by the miraculous flow of blood from a mother's heart to her unborn child. I know this by the flow of sap from the roots to the limbs of a tree, all the way to the very top. I know this through the flow of moisture from a tree's roots up through the trunk to each and every single leaf. I know this through the white and nourishing flow of milk from every human mother's breast, and from the breast of every mother creature.

Life is flowing... it never stops. When it ceases in one spot, it resumes somewhere else; forever, and ever, in an endless immortal blaze of Nature.

Embracing the Goddess

When you need personal power, when you need divine guidance, when you need protection or healing, when you need relief from mental anguish, when you need to connect with the divine on a personal universal huge in-your-face way... invoke Sophia.

Sophia's Correspondences

Herbs: Bittersweet, pine, sage, star anise, anise, slippery elm
Animal: Dove
Color: Yellow
Planet: Mercury
Day: Wednesday
Element: Air
Feminine Face: Mother

Thalia

Her Story

The Greek goddess Thalia is a goddess of vegetation and foliage, the "Blooming Goddess", one of the three Graces. Thalia is the goddess of springtime. She represents the earth's bounty, its abundance and fertility.

Thalia's Garden

Whether you live in a house with a nice-sized plot of land to till what you want for a garden space, or whether you are a city apartment dweller with only a balcony and some pots, you can create a magickal garden devoted to the goddess using the energy of Thalia. The following garden layout is equally do-able with both of the above scenarios. It'll work. It's about size and dimension and the relativity of it all.

At the Four Corners: Plant hibiscus, to honor the goddess and your own feminine energy and power.

To the North: Plant primroses, for the element of Earth. May they bring to you physical wellbeing and manifestation of your magick into the world of atoms and matter.

To the East: Plant sage, for the element of Air. May it bring to you mental wellbeing and manifestation of your magick into the world of the mind and its ever-winding labyrinth of thought.

To the South: Plant marigolds, for the element of Fire. May they bring to you all the energy you need for all the passion it will take to make a difference in this lifetime and beyond.

To the West: Plant asters, for the element of Water. May they bring to you inspiration in the form of dreams and spirit contact; inner sight; honest emotions; and a cleansing of your body, mind, and spirit.

And at the center of Thalia's garden, what do you plant?

Plant yourself. Stand, sit, or lay in this sacred center, absorbing the energies all around you, the energies of the elements, the energies of the plants, the energy of the goddess.

Embracing the Goddess

Thalia's energy can be invoked for your spring planting, or to celebrate spring and the sprouting of the world once more into a magickal green blossoming realm. Thalia can be invoked when abundance is needed, abundance on many levels: material things – money, food; immaterial things – *more...* more laughter, more spontaneity, more happiness, just "more"... whatever it may be.

Thalia's Correspondences

Herbs: Vervain, corn, knotweed, patchouli, wood sorrel
Color: Brown, green
Planet: (Gaia) Earth
Day: All seven
Element: Earth
Feminine Face: Maiden

White Buffalo Calf Woman

Her Story

White Buffalo Calf Woman influences agriculture, basic survival, and enrichment rituals and ceremonies. She embraces the nurturing side of our nature; she is what prods us to excel and succeed in the rough arena of the world. White Buffalo Calf Woman is who we invoke in rituals and ceremonies to honor the Mother in us all, the caretaker. It is her energy that is present in every woman holding a baby to her breast, raising a child, caring for the animals of the earth, sharing her life with a man. This goddess is what compels us to place another person's wellbeing before our own.

Women Surviving the Modern World

1. Start each day with a small ritual. It doesn't have to be complicated – light a candle, or anoint yourself with an oil, or be still for a 5-minute meditation, or write down a thought in your journal.
2. When you become frustrated with the circumstances you are dealing with, put everything on hold for a half an hour and have a Starbucks. Yes, you are worth a $5 cup of coffee. You're worth a gazillion $5 cups of coffee.
3. Take a solitary walk in a favorite spot, or take a walk with your best friend, or take a walk with your dog – who just might be your best friend.
4. Watch a movie that inspires you, that makes you laugh; or watch a movie that makes you cry... even though you'll think you're crying because of the movie, you're really not, you're cleansing yourself from bottled up emotion.
5. Do something creative: If you write, start a book, even if this means writing just the first sentence in an empty

notebook, just one sentence, and you've started a book, more will come later. If you paint, start a painting, even if this means painting a canvas all over with one color; call it the background, and eventually you'll think of things to put on top of it. If you sculpt, pick up a lump of clay, even if all you do is roll it in the palm of your hands to form a ball, and call it good; eventually the ball will turn into something else.

6. Give away something to someone who needs it. Soon after you do this, you'll feel all warm and fuzzy inside. This is the Universe, rushing back at you with positive energy and lots and lots of *Love*.

7. Clean out your refrigerator. You won't really just be cleaning out your refrigerator, you'll be cleaning out all the unnecessary junk that's cluttering up your life. When you're all done (with the refrigerator), and you stand there holding the door open, admiring all the sparkling clean shelves and extra space, know that you're not just looking at a refrigerator.

8. Call someone who's lonely. The unexpected connection will jump start a chain reaction of positive energy. When you finish talking to this person, you'll feel an inrush of their energy, and then a burst of Sun-Rays-Are-Coming-Out-My-Fingertips feeling. This is magick.

9. Buy: a) a pair of earrings; b) a new lipstick; or c) a pair of shoes. This sounds so material, but what's wrong with that? Know that you're not just purchasing Stuff, you're creating an affirmation with a physical action. In reality, you're shouting to the Universe: "I'm worth it!"

10. Be the first one to say: "I love you" or "I'm sorry".

Embracing the Goddess

Invoke this goddess in rituals honoring the "Mother" aspect of the Goddess, as well as the human "Mother" in us all. For deep within us all, every individual has the capability to nurture. It's the print of humanity.

White Buffalo Calf Woman's Correspondences

Herbs: Quince, bistort, wheat, sage, hyssop

Animal: White buffalo

Color: White, purple, green, brown

Planet: Jupiter

Day: Thursday

Element: Earth

Feminine Face: Mother

Symbol: Buffalo

Part 2

Affirmations and Goals

Affirmations

The Physical Aspect

This is my body... No one shall touch this body without my express permission. No one shall impose upon my body a physical action, intention, criteria, procedure, or judgment, that I have not expressly approved. This is my body, created by the Mother Goddess in all the glory of her likeness. Whether this body be large or small, fit or weak; whether this body align with the cultural views and norms of my society or not: my body is beautiful and will be respected as such.

Questions for Introspection

The Physical

1. What is my best feature?
2. What are two things about my body I'd like to change?
3. What would I have to do to make these changes?
4. Realistically, would it be possible for me to do this, and if I could successfully make these changes, who would I be making them for?
5. Am I able to accept my physical body in its beautiful, natural state; am I able to embrace myself as I am?
6. Is my body healthy?
7. If not, what are my health issues?
8. What do I need to do in order to correct these issues, or just generally improve my health, strength, and endurance?
9. List three things you know are not healthy for you, but you do anyway.
10. List three things you do for yourself that contribute to your physical wellbeing.
11. What do I love most about my body?

The Spiritual Aspect

I will connect with the universe through the Divine Feminine, and through that connection with my ancestors and the root of all that is me...

For centuries the Divine Feminine has been ripped from the heart and soul of womanhood, shrouded in stories of evil encompassing snakes and apples, betrayal and guilt. Womanhood needs to wrestle its freedom from this lie, to regain its strength and equilibrium through the power of the Mother Goddess.

Through the youthful exuberance of the Maiden, the fertility of the Mother, and the wisdom of the Crone, we have to pass on to our daughters the beauty of the feminine mystique, impressing upon them the reverence and respect that is its due. While the world still revolves around the decisions of men, it is women who harvest its bounty through their children, their art, their writing, their dreams, and their strong sense of nurturing. It is woman who builds up; and through her spirituality and connection with the Goddess, woman can repair the damage of previous generations, building new futures and opportunities for her children.

With our strong and renewed sense of connection to the Feminine Divine, the most important thing we can do is to impart upon our fathers, husbands, brothers, and sons the strength, beauty, wisdom, and power of womanhood at its most pure. We can lead them back to the Goddess, who is, after all, their Mother too.

Questions for Introspection

The Spiritual

1. Do I feel a strong connection with Feminine Divinity?
2. How has the Goddess touched my life?
3. Do I feel free to embrace Goddess Spirituality openly?
4. If not, what are the obstacles to doing so?
5. Realistically, can these obstacles be overcome?

6. What do I do each day to connect with Spirit?
7. How has my connection to the Goddess and my spiritual practices enhanced my daily life?
8. List three things that you think impede your spiritual growth.
9. List three things that have inspired you during your life.
10. What do you love most about your spirituality right now?
11. Is there a woman you know who would benefit by learning about the Mother Goddess?

The Mental Aspect

I will not allow other people's opinions to form the image I carry of myself...

Whether these opinions are formed and passed on to me by friends, family, or foe; if these opinions are filled with negativity, if these opinions are laced with jealousy, spite, judgmental prejudice, ambiguity, cruelty, or ignorance, I will disregard these opinions. These opinions will be shed as a snake sheds its skin, leaving renewed vitality and beauty beneath, exposing my true nature, in tune with the Goddess and a healthy ego.

Questions for Introspection

The Mental

1. Do I expect too much of myself?
2. Do I feel like I have to be responsible for everyone?
3. Is there a lot of stress in your life right now?
4. If so, what are the main causes of this stress?
5. Realistically, can the circumstances or people causing this stress be resolved or dismissed from your life?
6. If so, what steps must you take to correct the issue?
7. Do you give yourself time to daydream?
8. When you are sad, what makes you happy?
9. What makes you laugh?

10. What makes you cry?
11. What are you afraid of?
12. Do you have someone in your life with whom you can share your deepest thoughts?

Goals

I will set goals to move my life forward: to celebrate achievements; to revel in accomplishments; to improve my circumstances; to embellish my femininity with wholesome activities; to render unto my daughters, granddaughters, nieces, and students a heritage of strength, beauty, stability, and radiance.

I asked women to send me a list of their goals. I received the following essays and notes from a variety of women in various life circumstances. They are all inspiring and uplifting. They shine a light upon womanhood and what makes us tick, what we strive for, what we desire, and how we think about ourselves:

I am Crone. My goal is to be High Priestess, and to teach others of the Goddess... gone through one year at Woolston-Stein Theological Seminary through Aquarian Tabernacle Church, now a Dedicant of SunCrow, who was Teacher there and is 3rd Degree HPS in TN. I hope to move there in spring to continue my studies. I am working on my First Degree now. I do have two Granddaughters of the Goddess, whom I will be teaching as they grow up.

I am a Crone. My goal is to become the woman I've always been meant to be, but have been too afraid to be. I'm getting there. I've been a practicing witch for a year and a half and Pagan born. My Grandmother was half Cherokee. I'm out of the broom closet in a big way, and my goals include serving the earth and the Goddess in every way I can be of use and to give the young Pagans and witches an example to follow.

I'm a mother. My goals are to get through life with as much happiness as I can get without stress. Another goal is to learn as much as I can about the gifts that were handed down to me by my grandfather. I never met him, but heard so much about him. It feels like it's something I need to do. My third goal is to take care of my mom to the best of my ability, so she will be comfortable and happy with the time she has left on this earth. A big goal that seems hard to achieve is to be happy for myself, as I want to make me happy, but I put everyone before myself.

I am now in the Crone stage (thanks to surgery and life, lol).

1. I will understand my past lives, I will get off the hamster wheel that I spent my Goddess (Mother stage) days upon.
2. I will embrace my gifts and understand how to use them to help more, instead of just tolerating them.
3. I will take notice of my health and fix what is wrong instead of just accepting it and putting it off.
4. I will finish up my schooling so I can get a better job.
5. I will get my financials in line (bankruptcy, better job, budget).
6. I will take the time to open my mind and be able to accept a mate into my life.
7. I will start doing more with my youngest son (getting him away from electronics). So when I go to bed, I know that I was the best mom I can be.

I have been an eclectic solitary witch from childhood to my now 70 years.
Goals now:

- To make the world a better place; nurture nature; share love, peace, and hope.

- To gain more knowledge on the path and to share.
- To prepare for the next journey on my soul's path, and to hopefully leave this incarnation with less karma.
- To widen my horizons in metaphysics and spirituality, and to share my knowledge.
- To use my gifts to help others.

I do believe that as the time approaches, we should be sure we know our soul and our purpose.

This is a bit of my goals... the list is huge.

As a mother of three sons, all a year apart, I look back on my years as a mother and wonder if I did it right. It wasn't easy, in fact, it was downright hard. I doubted myself a lot back then, and I doubted that I could do it very well. As my children have grown into men, I look at the kind of men they have become. I see brave, kind, generous, strong men. I guess I must have done something right somewhere along the way, and I'm very proud of them. My grandson, my greatest joy, is my chance to love with all my heart, because now it is wide open.

At age 38, I began early menopause. I have been in this stage of life for quite a while now; I'm 52. I have read of a fourth stage in a woman's life called the "Maga" stage or "Queen" stage. Since women are living much longer, this is a stage between the Mother and the Crone stages, the Mabon stage, if you will. I prefer this to the Crone, who seems to be so much older, far older than me. It means I can spend time for myself; I am coming into my own; I no longer worry about silly little things, caring what others think about me. I don't even know what that is anymore.

I was sidetracked from life for just a little while. I became ill. I have been very sick a couple of times. I've been so sick that it brought me to my knees. I could not do anything except go within myself to a very deep dark place. There, I learned that life is fragile, and I had taken it for granted. I had been too hard on myself, on my expectations of the future and my view of the world. I had to rewire the way I talked to myself, which wasn't easy. And one deep breath at a time, learn to treat myself with gentleness and kindness. I am here now, and that's all that matters.

As has been the case for most of this stage of my life, I would love to share my experiences and teach what I have learned. My attention turns towards the world and how fast it is changing. I can see now how the trials I have been through were a way of preparing me for this. That's how life works. And I'm sure there is more to come. I would love to make more videos about spirituality and Witchcraft. Perhaps even a documentary. Film-making seems to be my greatest passion.

At this point, I'm just riding the waves. We'll see where they take me.

I want to add to your "Crone" category! My two girls are grown now and have flown the coop, but I'm the one who feels like the bird who's just been let out of the cage! Since my tarot business has been taking off so wonderfully, I sold my house so that I wouldn't have the burden of it, and now I'm enjoying weighing my options. I can go anywhere, do anything, as long as I have internet access to do my work. I've been traveling around doing readings and selling cards, saving money so that if I find a place I'd like to land, I can just plop down. I've never felt this much freedom.

Goal: To keep this sense of airiness, keep working and creating, while still maintaining a wonderful relationship with my two beautiful talented daughters.

From a Mother: Success would be making a difference in the world and making enough money to enjoy our lives with our kids. We've already got projects started. We're waiting to raise capital on two of them.

Child rearing: I consider child rearing success to be that my kids have the platform for being the best versions of themselves they can be. It's a vague goal, but I think I'm doing well thus far.

The house: It's just needing some repairs – redo carpeting; remodel the bathroom; dry-wall needs replacement in some spots; painting; fixing up the patio; making a sitting nook patio on the front; fixing up the yard; repainting and remodeling the garage. This house has been my home since my parents bought it 25 years ago. It's home, but it needs a facelift. I want it to be a place that invokes a sense of pride in making it my own and a place that combines functionality with solid craftsmanship. It is my retreat, my public face, my creation, and my workshop.

A Mother: I am a 30-something mother of three beautiful, healthy children, a wife, a Chartered Herbalist, and a solitary witch. My goals at this stage in my life are to provide a positive and creative world for my kids, to educate them about the importance of being true to oneself – no matter what! With all the issues on bullying, peer pressure, etc., I know when people believe in themselves, anything can be accomplished!

I also believe in self-respect, family values, and not compromising oneself just for the sake of others. It's important to me to teach my children manners, self-discipline, and being grateful for each and every day. It's definitely not easy trying not to control them in every way (I'm kind of a control freak), and to allow them to have their own personalities.

Two of my children are Fire signs (like me), and my second

born is an Earth sign (he's really a breath of fresh air, being so mellow and relaxed), so I am frequently telling my oldest and youngest to relax and stay calm. My hubby is a Water sign. He's so laid back that I'm usually the one who is stressed out, but I know in my heart that all is well, and I'm doing the best I can. Providing my family with lots of love and happiness is so extremely important, and if they ever feel like no one understands, or the world is being unfair, I'm always there to listen and help them in any way I can.

Part 3

A Woman's Life Through the Elements

Earth, Through the Miracle
of our Physical Bodies

Earth Energy Affirmations

1. My body is beautiful.
2. I'm happy with my body at this weight. I'm shapely, curving, and delightfully feminine.
3. I embrace my monthly cycle as a connection to the earth, fertility, and the Goddess.
4. I embrace my monthly cycle and the blessed moon blood as a symbol of my womanhood and as an empowering magickal tool.
5. I revel in my ability to give birth and to nurture a child with my own body.
6. I revel in my sexuality, in sharing my body with my partner, as well as exploring and enjoying my body in solitude.
7. I embrace menopause and all it encompasses. I view it as a moment in life to seize and celebrate, for it is the continuation of an eternal journey.

Earth Invocation

Earth, Element of the North, you who encompass all things of the physical world, materialize for me in the form of early spring apple blossoms; hazelnut coffee; the soft fur of a tabby cat; the cold wet nose of a dog; and the pressure of a child's arms around my neck.

Air, Through the Miracle of our Creativity and Intelligence

Air Energy Affirmations

1. I am intelligent, and I shall let no one tell me otherwise.
2. I embrace my creative muse with passion, enthusiasm, and a promise to follow through on all projects.
3. I am a good listener, a strong shoulder to lean on, a well of compassion for friends and family in times of stress.
4. I freely embrace the concept of open communication, and I fervently strive to keep the lines of communication open between me, my friends, and family.
5. I express myself with passion, honesty, and eloquence.
6. I will allow no one to censor my beliefs, my opinions, or my speech.
7. I embrace the spirit of the fairies, dancing my own dance to my own tune.

Air Invocation

Air, Element of the East, you who encompass all thought and creativity, materialize for me in the form of long and eloquent letters to a far away friend; the magickal touch of my elusive muse; the musical notes of a favorite song; and the breathless words of a final farewell.

Fire, Through the Passion that is our Will

Fire Energy Affirmations

1. I will not allow my passion and enthusiasm for life to be diminished by the negative reaction of another.
2. I claim my personal space, and I cleanse this space of all negative energy.
3. I embrace my "passion of the moment", no matter what it might be, as a way for divinity to broaden my horizons.
4. I will not apologize for the fire in my soul.
5. I embrace the magick of the salamander, the creature of this element, as a cleansing and protective talisman.
6. I will allow the transforming heat and flames of fire to strengthen my will, as fire tempers and strengthens steel.
7. Fire, burn away that which encumbers me, those things in life that hold me back, all that curtails what I can accomplish.

Fire Invocation

Fire, Element of the South, you who encompass passion and transformation, materialize for me in the form of unbridled lust for a true love; a flaming thirst for justice; an unquenchable energy for living; and enthusiastic acceptance of life's ever-changing landscape.

Water, Through our Natural Intuition and Empathy

Water Energy Affirmations

1. I will embrace the Goddess within me.
2. I will listen to my intuition and trust my natural instinct.
3. I embrace my dreams, whether they be prophetic, a message from the other side, or life's everyday drivel... I shall learn something from them all.
4. I call upon the energy of Water to cleanse and purify my body, soul, and spirit.
5. I call upon the energy of Water to cleanse and purify my space.
6. I call upon the divine presence of this element, so keenly connected with the Goddess, to baptize me into the world of spiritual awareness.
7. I embrace the magickal mysteries of new-age awareness, learning from ancient hidden knowledge the ways of my ancestors, the ways of my sisters.

Water Invocation

Water, Element of the West, you who hold the esoteric mysteries of the mind and the energy of the Goddess, materialize for me in the form of sweet dreams; visions and intuition pure enough to assist those in need; a deeper understanding of Women's Mysteries; and a cleansing of the Spirit from the mundane baggage of the world.

Part 4

A Woman's Life Through the Year

As the year progresses and time passes, so a woman's life progresses with it, changing with the seasons, not only the seasons of nature, but the seasons of life itself and all that each stage encompasses. A woman will go through a monumental transition about every twenty years: from maiden, to married woman (motherhood and child-rearing), and in the last stage possibly widowhood and solitude. But in between each major milestone our lives are sprinkled with a myriad of life altering moments and a baptism by the Goddess on a day-to-day basis. As Mother Earth, a material manifestation of the Goddess, goes through impregnation (spring); growth (summer); harvest (autumn); and death (winter), she grabs us by the hand and drags us along for the ride, kicking and screaming all the way, evolving into the women we were meant to be, living the lives that are our destiny.

The following are a list of pagan holidays with the focus on the Goddess and her natural transitions, highlighting the concept of how women's lives run a parallel course that leads to an awakening of the Divine Feminine and an awakening to our own soul nature. You will also discover in this section ways to celebrate the holidays, ways to incorporate the meanings and symbolism into your own life, whatever path you may be on, whatever stage you may be in. Included in this section are my own personal thoughts and traditions for each holiday, along with recipes and anecdotes. What you will not find in this section are formal written religious rituals reminiscent of mainstream religious services meant to be recited by rote. That's not the way we celebrate these holidays at my house.

So what is the significance of these holidays to the modern pagan? Why do we still celebrate them, and what do they mean to us?

I think, for one thing, we have some innate deep-seated unspoken need to have our lives punctuated by milestones; whether personal milestones like weddings, graduations, and births; or societal, communal, and spiritual milestones. There's a strange reassurance that the universe works in an ordered and predictable manner and timetable. And maybe this is comforting to us because so much of life is unexpected, unpredictable, played without a script, and undeniably finite.

Long after we are but a memory, there will still be people celebrating these pagan holidays, punctuating the end of summer, welcoming with open arms the predictable end to the season of light and warmth, retreating into the dark and comforting confines of winter and the still peace that it will bring, only to return to a new season of light with spring.

Every season, and every seasonal celebration, holds its own kind of magick and adds to our lives in a way that helps us explore the possibilities, survive the inevitable, and move toward the future.

Samhain (October 31)

The Goddess is old and wizened. She's settling into this stage of her persona to reap the benefit of all that she has experienced, all that has transpired on her journey to this point. She's preparing for the dark months, gathering her harvest about her, both for her physical survival and her emotional revival, using this time to rest, to gather energy for the future and the light that she knows will return. On this phase of her journey she can afford to sit back in quiet reflection, to shed those things in her life that have become a burden, and to look forward to the end of her journey, or rather, the beginning of the next.

Samhain (pronounced "Sou-wen") is a celebration that has a more somber side than the revelry of modern Halloween. It is a day of remembrance of your ancestors and for those family members who have passed over. Pagan families may set an extra place at the supper table on this evening, to honor those loved ones who are no longer with them. The veil between the world of the living and the dead is thinnest on this eve, and this night is an excellent time to perform divination, or to try to connect with those spirits from the other side.

My Celebration

Samhain is a big deal at our house. Some years ago we began the tradition of a bonfire in the front driveway, an open house for friends, children's friends, and acquaintances. You'll find a table set up by the fire pit for a weenie roast, with smores for dessert. In the kitchen, I've got a large kettle of chili on the stove, and a large kettle of hot apple cider. Costumes are optional, for those who are comfortable dressing up, I say go for it; for those who are not, don't sweat it. And, of course, there will be a large bowl of candy for the children in our neighborhood who follow the age-old custom of trick or treating.

You always hear that the veil has thinned on this night and spirit contact is almost inevitable if one wishes to put forth some effort. Samhain is also reputed to be a superb night for divination of any kind, and with this in mind, I set up a table on the back porch full of divination tools: tarot cards, rune stones, pendulums, oriental divination sticks, and don't forget the Ouija board for those who wish to try their hand at communing with the spirits. Guests seem to love this opportunity, and there will be people seated around this table off and on all evening. It gives many a chance to learn about, touch, and use divination tools that they may not be familiar with and might otherwise not have access to.

Samhain Correspondences

Herbs: Patchouli, sage, heather

Altar Flowers/Herbs: Acorns, apples, pumpkins/gourds, dittany, autumn leaves

Feast Foods: Pumpkin, squash, nut breads, sweet potatoes, mulled drinks (cider, wine), roast meat, root vegetables

Animals: Bats, cats, crows, ravens, owls

Incense: Cinnamon, cloves, myrrh, patchouli, pine, mugwort, nutmeg

Rituals/Spells: Making besoms, divination, spirit contact, crone magick, working with dark energy, spells for new beginnings

Samhain Recipes

My Pumpkin Pie

Ingredients:

1 16 oz. can pumpkin (about 2 cups)

1 13 oz. can evaporated milk (but sometimes I use sweetened condensed milk – it makes it more "chiffony"... is that a word?)

2 eggs

½ cup brown sugar

½ sugar

The Spices:
Cinnamon, ginger, nutmeg, allspice, cloves, and a dash of salt. Most recipes call for ½ teaspoon each, but I'm much more generous with my spices!

The Crust:
I tried for years to learn to make a good pie crust, and I almost gave up out of frustration, then I found this recipe. It's almost fool-proof, no kidding.

Ingredients:
2 ½ cups flour
1 teaspoon salt
1 cup shortening
1 beaten egg
1 tablespoon vinegar
¼ cup water

Mix the dry ingredients together and cut in the shortening, as usual. Then combine the egg and vinegar, stirring it up a bit, and add this to your dry ingredients. Add the water a dash at a time as you work it in, you'll be able to tell when you get a good texture.

Bake at 400 degrees for the first 15 minutes, and at 350 degrees for the next 30-40 minutes. When you can stick a butter knife in the center of the pie, and it comes out clean, your pie is done.

Hot Apple Cider
I have a *huge* – did I say huge? – kettle that I use to mix up my cider. This sits and simmers all afternoon on the backburner of my stove, wafting a wonderful aroma throughout the house.

Ingredients:
5-7 large jugs of apple juice
8-10 bags of peach tea
A handful of cinnamon sticks
A large metal tea ball filled with whole cloves and allspice

You can leave a shaker of nutmeg sitting on the counter and anyone who wants to add a dash of this spice to their mug of apple cider can do so.

If you don't like this cider full force, you can dilute it some with water to suit your own taste.

The Winter Solstice: Yule (December 21)

The Goddess, pregnant with life experiences, gives birth to her future, continuing life's unending cycle, renewing the universe with new dreams and infinite possibilities. As the light returns to the earth on the Winter Solstice in a glorious burst from the sun, so our light shines through the Goddess, illuminating our way, igniting our path with energy, ambition, and a renewed sense of purpose.

Winter Solstice... the longest day of darkness in the year; and with the darkness comes the promise of light, the rebirth of the sun. It's no wonder, because of the importance of this date to the ancient pagans and the symbolism involved, that the Roman Catholic church chose this date to celebrate the birth of Christ. This is a celebration of sunshine. It's celebrating the end of darkness and cold; it's celebrating a return to the earth and warmth, a return to gardening, a return of the flowers, a return of warm sunny days, green grass, ice cream, and lazy afternoons fishing at the lake. It might be a way off yet, but it's coming, really it is, and the Winter Solstice will keep its promise!

Hallelujah, the sun has returned!

My Celebration

When the kids were younger, not all that long ago in fact, I use to start shopping for Yule in August. Yes, I really did. I also carried a notebook in my purse with everyone's name so that I could keep track of everything I was buying for each child. Of course, I firmly believed that everyone must have the same amount of gifts to open; I was adamant about that. And I was so organized, in fact, that I kept this notebook with me all through the gift wrapping process to check off which presents were completed. I wore myself out. I wore my bank account out; and I discovered that I actually wore my kids out with this process as well. One

124

day, my youngest daughter said to me, "Mom, it's so stressful. I just get my room the way I want it, then we get all this stuff, and it's all cluttered again, and I have to find somewhere to put it all." That was an eye-opening moment.

I have shifted my concentration to preparing a good meal for the family.

I've shifted my concentration to creating an atmosphere of congeniality, fun, and camaraderie. I've taken the commercial burden off myself and my children and, in doing so, we can all relax and come away with the most important holiday gift of all... happy memories.

Yule Correspondences

Herbs: Frankincense, myrrh, sage, bayberry, rosemary

Altar Flowers/Herbs: Holly, mistletoe, pine cones, evergreen, thistle, cedar

Feast Foods: Fruitcake, gingerbread, cranberries, dried fruit, eggnog, cider/wine

Animals: White buffalo, stag, weasels, owls, squirrels, blue jays, cardinals, doves

Incense: Bayberry, cedar, frankincense, myrrh, orange, sage, rosemary

Rituals/Spells: Hearth and home magick, lighting the Yule log, hopes and dreams spells, wishes

Yule Recipes

Gingerbread

Ingredients:

2 ½ cups flour

1 cup molasses

½ cup sugar

½ cup shortening

1 egg

1 ½ teaspoon baking soda
1 teaspoon cinnamon
1 teaspoon ginger
¾ teaspoon salt
½ teaspoon ground cloves
1 cup boiling water

In a large bowl, measure all the ingredients. With a mixer at low speed, beat until well mixed, constantly scraping the bowl with a rubber spatula. Beat at medium speed for 3 minutes. Pour the batter into a pan and bake for 55-60 minutes at 350 degrees.

We'll look at some of the ingredients now from a magickal perspective:

Cinnamon: Spirituality, success, healing, power, psychic powers, lust, protection, love
Ginger: Love, money, success, power
Salt: Purification, protection, grounding, money
Cloves: Protection, exorcism, love, money
Sugar: Love, lust

Cranberry/Orange Sauce
Ingredients:
2 (8 ounce) packages cranberries, fresh or frozen
1 orange, cut into strips and juiced
½ cup sugar
1 cinnamon stick

Put all the ingredients into a saucepan over medium heat and simmer until the cranberries burst and the sauce thickens, about 15 to 20 minutes. Serve at room temperature or cool and refrigerate. Remove the cinnamon stick before serving.

Imbolc (February 2)

The Goddess celebrates renewed fertility, fertility of body, mind, and spirit. Seeds are sown now for future harvests; the bricks and mortar of new paths and new adventures are laid. The Goddess is reborn as her younger self, the Maiden, and it is her strength and power and sinewy young muscle that we imbue ourselves with, so as to have the strength and endurance to fulfill our life journey.

This is also a festival of the Celtic goddess, Brighid (or Bride), so beloved by the people of the old world that the Roman Church couldn't eradicate her. Instead, they made her a saint, Saint Brigit. In Celtic lore, the Old Woman of Winter (the Cailleach) was reborn as Brighid/Bride, the Young Maiden of Spring. It's this image that is most prominent in my mind, from the halls of Catholic Parochial School, the beautiful shining faces of the female saints, innocently biding their time among the patriarchal rhetoric, waiting for the Great Awakening... St. Brigit most prominent among them (the nuns adored her).

The celebration of Imbolc is also a celebration of light, a celebration of the sun, in the fact that a successful new growing season depends upon it. The light and warmth of the sun are celebrated in the flames of candles and bonfires.

My Celebration

This milestone passes all but unnoticed at our house, in all truth. I touch on it with a public comment and picture at social sites, or among my pagan internet friends; but here, it's like a soft shadow passing over the house, sometimes lit with the glow of a blue candle on the kitchen table that hardly anyone else notices, since I'm always burning candles it seems. But I notice, and I remember, and I think... The time of The Great Awakening has come.

Imbolc Correspondences

Herbs: Basil, bay, celandine, benzoic

Altar Flowers/Herbs: Angelica, myrrh, flowers that are yellow/white/or blue

Feast Foods: Bread, cakes, dairy products, seeds

Animals: Burrowing animals, ewes, deer, goats, lambs

Incense: Jasmine, myrrh, neroli

Rituals/Spells: Candle magick, initiation, hearth/home blessings, fertility magick, healing magick, cleansing rituals

Imbolc Recipes

Creamed Cabbage

Ingredients:

1 lb. pre-cooked ham, 1 inch cubed or shredded

1 heaping teaspoon flour

1 firm white cabbage

½ teaspoon each salt and pepper

1 cup cream

Grated nutmeg (optional)

Cut the cabbage in half, then cut the halves once again. Drop them into a pot of boiling water and cook for 5 minutes, drain. Slice them up. Melt a little butter or margarine in a saucepan and add the shredded cabbage. Stir it up good. Add salt, pepper, and a dash of grated nutmeg. Next add the cream and a heaping teaspoon of flour, still stirring, and let it come to a boil. Add the cubed or shredded ham, and lower the heat. Cover the saucepan and let the mixture simmer for about 30 minutes. Serve hot. Makes 6-8 servings.

Interestingly enough, and just as a side note, *nutmeg* is the most popular herb used to induce fidelity in a romantic partner. Think about this, *when used with magickal intention*, if you're making this dish for your husband, boyfriend, fiancé, etc. ("This is a perfect example of a little innocent kitchen witchery in the making," she says with a wicked grin.)

Brigit's Biscuits
Ingredients:
2 ¼ cup Bisquick
⅓ cup milk
⅓ cup honey

Preheat the oven to 400 degrees Fahrenheit. Spray a baking sheet with non-stick spray or line with parchment paper. In a bowl, combine all the ingredients. Drop by tablespoon onto a baking sheet, 2 inches apart. Bake for 10-12 minutes until golden. Serve warm with butter.

The Spring Equinox: Ostara (March 21)

The Goddess manifests her treasures in the material world, and Mother Earth marks this event with the emergence of plants and young animals, setting the stage once again for future harvests, both those of the physical world and those of the spiritual realm. The miracle of birth is highlighted, and the miracle that is womanhood confirmed. Within the celebration of Ostara, fertility is emphasized and celebrated. Nature's womb, filled with the seeds of life, embellishes the earth in productivity and prosperity.

Ostara is a day when the period of light and dark are equal, heralding springtime planting and the promise of warmth returning for the summer months. Sunlight is going to reign supreme starting the very next day, second by second, minute by minute. This is also a celebration of the Saxon goddess of fertility... Eostre. Eggs and rabbits are symbols belonging to this goddess and are incorporated into the festivities and celebrations. Sound familiar yet? It's all about bunnies, fertile eggs, and growing things. Now's the time to start those seedlings in egg cartons, time to start planning your herb garden, digging out those pots and diving into a bag of potting soil. Smell the earth women, get your fingernails dirty, follow that natural instinct that you know is there, the one you've probably been trying to ignore... Grow things!

A noteworthy tidbit: *Easter is always celebrated on the first Sunday after the first full moon after the Spring Equinox.*

(The Goddess is smiling now.)

My Celebration

The biggest part of Ostara for my family has always been coloring Easter Eggs (we decorate about 4 or 5 dozen – often with witches, animals, and other very un-Eastery images). The magickal nocturnal visit of the Easter Bunny is also a yearly tradition at our house, complete with pretty baskets of goodies. With seven children, putting all those baskets together, dividing all that candy, has been quite a process.

But this celebration has a deeper meaning for me, one that was made indelible upon my soul. The year was 1969, I was 12 years old, and it was the traditional Christian Easter Sunday that my family was celebrating:

The night before, my Aunt was glowing – beautiful and striking looking at 32. She was helping my sister and me color Easter eggs, finishing up by combining all the colors to get an interesting brown egg. I'll never forget the sight of her holding the egg up in the air so we could all get a look at it, laughing out loud. This was to be the last truly happy day this woman would know for a very long time to come. The next day, her husband (my uncle) would suffer a massive heart attack and die in her arms in the foyer of their home. It was just after a beautiful Easter Sunday meal, and we were all there.

Every year since, when we color eggs for this spring celebration, I remember coloring eggs with my aunt the night before Easter Sunday 1969. It's a crystal-clear memory 44 years later. The symbolism of this holiday is brought home to me in the idea of rejuvenation, resurrection, a return to life – life in the form of warmth, sunshine, growing plants, small animals, and souls.

"Everything is connected," the Goddess is telling me.

Ostara Correspondences

Herbs: Cinquefoil, rose, violets, tansy, celandine
Altar Flowers/Herbs: Honeysuckle, iris, lily, daffodil, crocus
Feast Foods: Eggs, fish, honey, sweet food, leafy vegetables
Animals: Chicks, hares, rabbits, swallows
Incense: Honeysuckle, jasmine, lavender, lotus, magnolia, rose, violet

Rituals/Spells: Planting/sowing, rejuvenation spells, consecration of tools, grounding work, earth blessings, spring cleansing

Ostara Recipes

Magickal Egg Salad
Ingredients:
6 hard-boiled eggs, sliced
¼ cup mayonnaise
2 tsp. fresh lemon juice
1 tbsp. minced onion
¼ tsp. salt
¼ tsp. pepper
½ cup finely chopped celery
Lettuce leaves

Reserve four center egg slices for garnish, if desired. Chop the remaining eggs. Mix the mayonnaise, lemon juice, onion, salt and pepper in medium bowl. Add the chopped eggs and celery; mix well. Refrigerate, covered, to blend the flavors.

Serve on lettuce leaves; garnish with the reserved egg slices.

Honey Baked Ham
Ingredients:
18 to 20 pound smoked ham, water added, ham hock removed
One 16 ounce box light brown sugar
1 cup (8 ounce jar) clover honey

Adjust the oven racks to accommodate a large covered roasting pan. Fit the pan with a shallow rack. Preheat the oven to 350 degrees F.

Unwrap the ham and rinse it in cold water. Place it on the rack in the roasting pan. Cover the pan with the lid and bake for half the estimated cooking time. (Total cooking time is about 20 minutes per pound.) Halfway through the estimated cooking time, add the sugar and honey to a saucepan, cooking over medium heat until it is smooth and the sugar has dissolved. Pour the mixture over the ham and continue baking the ham, basting occasionally with the drippings in the roaster.

Check for doneness at the end of the estimated cooking time by inserting a meat thermometer at a meaty point (not into fat or touching the bone). It should register 160 degrees F.

Allow the ham to stand for 15 minutes before slicing to allow the juices to set.

Beltaine (May 1)

The Goddess celebrates sexuality, the joy of human copulation, and the soul connections that are created by this physical act. This holiday embraces the joy of the union, the idea of two (the God and the Goddess) becoming one, and celebrating the energy this union generates. As divinity embraces the physical and spiritual beauty of sex, so should we.

This holiday is one of the most pagan. It is a celebration of fertility and the sexuality that goes right along with it. To the modern world, it's more commonly known as May Day. What the Roman Catholic Church tried so hard to control, to portray as evil, sinful, or dirty is the very thing celebrated at Beltaine... human sexuality.

In modern celebrations of May Day, people still dance around the Maypole (some not realizing that this is a phallic symbol), while they hold brightly colored streamers spilling from the top of this pole, symbolic of the creative force of sex. In ancient days bonfires would roar through the night, dancing and merriment would ensue, and young lovers would steal away to the forest, to greet the dawn of a new day in each other's arms.

My Celebration

This is another one of those holidays that passes by quietly at our house, except for one very magickal practice.

It is said that at sunrise on the morning of Beltaine, those women wishing to recapture their youth, as well as all women wishing to retain their beauty, should go out into the grass at the break of dawn, sweep up the morning dew with their hands, and bathe their faces with it.

The ironic aspect of this practice is that, from a very little girl on, I use to do this quite regularly: step outside into the backyard, glance at the morning sun, sweep up dew from the grass into both hands, and bathe my face in it. Why would a child do this? It makes me wonder about all the natural, instinctual, and often unusual, things we do. It makes me wonder about all the magick buried deep within our subconscious, all the ancient ancestral knowledge that is part of our DNA. It makes me wonder what happened in the universe, in this vast world, that made us forget this magick?

And what has awakened this magick within us now?

Beltaine Correspondences

Herbs: Cinquefoil, frankincense, marigold, meadowsweet, woodruff
Altar Flowers/Herbs: Daisy, hawthorn, lilac, primrose, wildflowers, rose
Feast Foods: Barley cakes, oat cakes, red fruit, elderflower drinks, herbal salads
Animals: Honey bees, cats, horses, rabbits, white cows
Incense: Frankincense, lilac, passion flower, rose, vanilla
Rituals/Spells: Bale fire, fertility magick, sex magick, handfasting, beauty magick, love spells, the Great Rite

Beltaine Recipes

Strawberry/Rhubarb Pie
Ingredients for the crust:
2 cups all-purpose flour, plus additional flour as needed, up to ¼ cup
½ cup cake flour (recommended: Soft As Silk)
3 teaspoons sifted powdered sugar
½ cup butter-flavored shortening (recommended: Crisco)
¼ cup salted butter
Pinch of salt
1 egg
2 teaspoons vinegar
¼ cup ice-cold water

Ingredients for the filling:
2 ½ cups chopped red rhubarb, fresh
2 ½ cups de-stemmed, washed and cut strawberries (in larger pieces)
1 ½ cups sugar (1 ¼ cups for high altitude)
2 tablespoons minute tapioca
1 tablespoon all-purpose flour
½ teaspoon lemon zest
½ teaspoon lemon juice
½ teaspoon ground cinnamon
1 teaspoon vanilla extract
3 tablespoons butter, cubed small
1 egg white beaten with 1 teaspoon water
Large granule sugar

Making the crust:
Using 2 pastry blenders, blend the flours, sugar, shortening, butter and salt. Whisk the egg, vinegar, and water in a 2-cup measure and pour over the dry ingredients, incorporating all the liquid without overworking the dough. Toss the additional flour over the ball of dough and chill if possible. Divide the dough into 2 disks. Roll out 1 piece of dough to make a bottom crust. Place into a pie dish. Put the dish in a refrigerator to chill.

Preheat the oven to 425 degrees Fahrenheit.

Making the filling:
Mix the rhubarb, strawberries, sugar, tapioca, flour, zest and juice of lemon, dash of cinnamon, and vanilla. Mix well in a large bowl and pour out into chilled crust. Dot the top of the filling with the butter. Brush the edges of the pie crust with egg white wash. Roll out the other piece of dough and place over the filling. Crimp to seal the edges. Brush with egg white wash and garnish with large granule sugar. Bake at 425

degrees Fahrenheit for 15 minutes. Decrease the temperature to 375 degrees Fahrenheit and bake for an additional 45 to 50 minutes.

Let it cool before serving.

Lusty Chocolate Mousse
Ingredients:
5 ¼ ounces bittersweet chocolate, coarsely chopped
14 ounces cold heavy cream
3 large egg whites
1 ounce sugar
Sweetened whipped cream, for garnish, optional
Shaved bittersweet chocolate, for garnish, optional

Place the chocolate in a large bowl set over a bain-marie or in a double boiler at a low simmer. Stir the chocolate until melted. Turn off the heat and let it stand.

Beat the cream over ice until it forms soft peaks. Set aside and hold at room temperature. With a mixer, whip the egg to soft peaks. Gradually add the sugar and continue whipping until firm.

Remove the chocolate from the bain-marie and, using a whisk, fold in the egg whites all at once. When the whites are almost completely incorporated, fold in the whipped cream. Cover the mousse and refrigerate for approximately 1 hour or until set. Serve in goblets topped with more whipped cream and shaved chocolate, if desired... Yum!

The Summer Solstice: Litha (June 21)

Midsummer's Eve, the longest day of the year. This holiday, steeped in fairy lore, is a magickal time filled with the earth's bounty. Gardens, fields, and forests are blooming with productivity, overflowing with abundant fertility and the promise of rich harvests to come. As the earth is pregnant with summer's lush growth, so too is the Goddess, pregnant with new energy, infinite possibilities, and the promise of a rich spiritual harvest.

It's all about the fairies, this celebration, this pagan holiday. Fairy contact is generally easier to achieve on this day, for those of you who are brave enough to invoke the mischievous little folk, that is. But don't be surprised if soon afterwards you can't find your favorite earrings, or the car keys, or any other shiny inviting objects you may have left laying around. They are fickle, unpredictable, light-fingered creatures, a loaded gun. If you do decide to invoke the wee folk, you should know that there is a physical reaction you could experience when they appear. Your skin may feel "crawly", as though there were ants or bugs walking on you. This isn't harmful, and you will be perfectly okay, in spite of the ick factor. It will just be a cue to you that your invocation was successful.

If you prefer to avoid fairies, you should know that they detest iron. To keep them at bay, lay iron nails in the four corners of your house, or your property, keep iron kettles in your kitchen, witches – keep your cast iron cauldrons out in the open. Fairies will avoid *you*.

This all being said, know that fairies heal... *they heal*. Call upon them when you need them without fear.

June is a popular month for weddings, though few in the Christianized world realize why. The Druids celebrated the Summer Solstice as the "marriage between heaven and earth", and thus the popular belief that June is a "lucky" month for marriage ceremonies. There will be pagan spirit gatherings all around the world at this time, the most famous and the most notable at Stonehenge, where large groups of people will gather to celebrate and stay up all night in order to welcome the dawn.

My Celebration

For several years, all during my son's childhood, there has been one very special tradition at our house connected with the celebration of Litha.

When my son was a little boy, he used to like to stay up through the "Witching Hour" and watch for fairies. He'd get comfy in his pjs and robe. I'd gather up a lawn chair and place it beneath the large apple tree in our yard; and I'd prepare a special candle, placing it in a fire-proof receptacle along with some herbs to offer the fairies. It was his time to sit quietly outside in the dark and watch for these magickal creatures, the only light being that of the candle and the moon, if it were out.

Most of the time, these evenings were uneventful, but one Midsummer's Eve, my son's patience was rewarded.

From across the lawn, he saw what he said looked like three very small blue lights dancing along the top of the fence. Eventually these three tiny lights dropped from the fence to the lawn beneath, where they bounced around in the grass for several seconds, and then they disappeared. My son came back to the house breathless and wide-eyed to tell me what he had seen.

The next morning, we went out to investigate the grass where the lights had been. Overnight, three mushrooms had popped up to create a perfectly formed triangle in this area, and the grass in the middle of this formation was withered and yellowed.

I can't tell you with 100% accuracy whether what my son saw were fairies or not, but that really doesn't matter. All that really matters is that one little boy had a very magickal and memorable night.

Litha Correspondences

Herbs: Fennel, lavender, chamomile, cinquefoil, mugwort, thyme
Altar Flowers/Herbs: Larkspur, rose, wisteria, St. John's wort
Feast Foods: Apples, citrus, fruits, ale, mead, honey cakes
Animals: Butterflies, frogs, toads, wrens
Incense: Ylang ylang, thyme, rose, sandalwood, chamomile
Rituals/Spells: All-night fairy vigils, candle magick, dream work, familiar blessings, herb gathering, self-dedication, sun magick

Litha Recipes

Strawberry Shortcake
Ingredients:
3 pints fresh strawberries
½ cup white sugar
2 ¼ cups all-purpose flour
4 teaspoons baking powder
2 tablespoons white sugar
¼ teaspoon salt
⅓ cup shortening
1 egg
⅔ cup milk
2 cups whipped heavy cream

Slice the strawberries and toss them with ½ cup of white sugar. Set aside.

Preheat oven to 425 degrees F (220 degrees C). Grease and flour one 8 inch round cake pan.

In a medium bowl combine the flour, baking powder, 2 tablespoons white sugar and the salt. With a pastry blender cut in the shortening until the mixture resembles coarse crumbs. Make a well in the center and add the beaten egg and milk. Stir until just combined.

Spread the batter into the prepared pan. Bake at 425

degrees F (220 degrees C) for 15 to 20 minutes or until golden brown. Let it cool partially in the pan on a wire rack.

Slice the cooled cake in half, making two layers. Place half of the strawberries on one layer and top with the other layer. Top with the remaining strawberries and cover with the whipped cream.

Fairy Punch

Ingredients:

1 (64 fluid ounce) bottle fruit punch, chilled
1 (64 fluid ounce) bottle unsweetened pineapple juice, chilled
1 (2 liter) bottle ginger ale, chilled
½ gallon orange sherbet

In a punch bowl, mix together the fruit punch, pineapple juice and ginger ale. Add scoops of sherbet into the punch. Wait for the sherbet to begin melting, which should take approximately 10 minutes, stir gently, and serve.

Lammas (August 1)

As the matron of ancient times would start early to prepare her family for the harsh winter months ahead, so the Mother Goddess prepares us. She reminds us of the bounty yet to come with an early harvest of grain. She encourages us to take stock of what we have, and this pertains to the physical harvests, of course, but it can also include taking stock of ourselves, re-evaluating our goals, our lives, our paths, our relationships, our strengths, and our weaknesses.

This is the first of the harvest festivals, and in the ancient world this was indeed a time of celebration. A successful harvest would mean survival in the harsh winter months. In the northern countries this was, in particular, a celebration of the first harvest of wheat, thus bread is featured in the celebration of Lammas, also known as Lughnasadh.

As the modern day pagans celebrate this festival they will build roaring bonfires, feed each other a mouthful of bread, and with wine they will toast each other: *"May you eat the bread of life."*

My Celebration

Yes, it's a harvest festival. Yes, bread and wheat, as well as other grains, figure into it. But for me, it was more about the passage of time. It's about how time plays tricks on us, and as a child on summer vacation from school, these three months seemed like a whole year rolled up into one magickal moment.

August 1 in South Dakota meant lots of lingering blistering summer days ahead, the heat being almost as intense as July; but it also meant something different in the air, that faint scent (an autumn scent), a nuance of change in the sunlight, the slight tinge starting at the edge of the leaves. And then one morning, being greeted with crisp air and a sky so blue it was almost painful to look at, so beautiful it was.

This holiday, this moment in time, is a mystery. It is the ability to look back into the past while standing on some invisible magickal horizon so that you can see the future, but just enough of the future to tease you forward. *And you come to this exact same time and place year after year.* August 1, another summer coming to a close, one of so many, and another autumn returning. An end, to make way for something new to begin, again, and again, and again.

The figure standing on the horizon grows, matures, changes, morphs, ages, expands, learns, regrets, loves, hates, wonders, questions, fears, laughs, and listens. The figure on the horizon passes through a human lifetime in the blink of an eye, with one inaudible breath... and then they fade into an ethereal creature of smokey wisps with a voice that is but the wind.

Lammas Correspondences

Herbs: Frankincense, wheat, cornstalks, heather

Altar Flowers/Herbs: Corn ears, hollyhock, myrtle, oak leaves, wheat

Feast Foods: Apples/apple pie, cornbread, sweet potatoes/sweet potato pie, grapes, blackberries

Animals: Calves, roosters, deer

Incense: Chamomile, rose, rosemary, allspice, sandalwood, carnation

Rituals/Spells: Maternal magick, prosperity spells, purification spells, thanksgiving rituals, career spells

Lammas Recipes

Lemon Poppy Seed Muffins (with Glaze)

Ingredients for the muffins:

⅔ cup sugar

Grate 2 lemons

Juice of 1 lemon

2 cups all-purpose flour
2 teaspoons baking powder
¼ teaspoon baking soda
¼ teaspoon salt
¾ cup sour cream
2 large eggs
1 ½ teaspoons pure vanilla extract
1 stick (8 tablespoons) unsalted butter, melted and cooled
2 tablespoons poppy seeds

Ingredients for the icing:
1 cup confectioners' sugar, sifted
2-3 tablespoons fresh lemon juice

Center a rack in the oven and preheat the oven to 400 degrees F. Line 12 molds in a regular-size muffin pan with paper muffin cups. Place the muffin pan on a baking sheet.

Banana Bread
Ingredients:
1 ¼ cups sugar
½ cup butter or margarine, softened
2 eggs
1 ½ cups mashed very ripe bananas (3 to 4 medium)
½ cup buttermilk
1 teaspoon vanilla
2 ½ cups all-purpose flour
1 teaspoon baking soda
1 teaspoon salt
1 cup chopped nuts, if desired

Move the oven rack to a low position so that the tops of the pans will be in the center of oven. Heat the oven to 350 degrees F. Grease the bottoms only of 2 loaf pans, 8½ x 4½ x

2½ inches, or 1 loaf pan, 9 x 5 x 3 inches.

Mix the sugar and butter in large bowl. Stir in the eggs until well blended. Add the bananas, buttermilk and vanilla. Beat until smooth. Stir in the flour, baking soda and salt until just moistened. Stir in the nuts. Pour into pans.

Bake 8-inch loaves about 1 hour, 9-inch loaf about 1 ¼ hours, or until a toothpick inserted in the center comes out clean. Cool for 10 minutes. Loosen the sides of the loaves from the pans; remove from pans and place top side up on a wire rack. Cool completely, for about 2 hours, before slicing.

The Autumnal Equinox:
Mabon (September 21)

The Goddess, in the death throes of the growing season, is at her most beautiful. As she moves towards the final harvest, in preparation for the dark days to come, she shines with the brilliance and color that are mirrored in the physical world as golden leaves, ripened fruit, withering vines, and frost-covered grass. The spiritual aspect of this stage is one that is just as beautiful, emphasizing once more the idea of completion and accomplishment, of finding that moment within development that culminates with depths of wisdom and the light of knowledge.

This day brings equal hours of light and dark, a second celebration of perfect equality. Beyond this day, light will gradually fade as the dark season descends upon the world. At this time of year, the ancient Druids would burn a large human-like wicker figure as part of their celebration. This figure represented the vegetation spirit, and indeed, the heralding of the dark season would bring an end to the growth and flowering of summer.

Modern pagans may celebrate this holiday with many of the foods connected with this time of year in their area. Decorations may include leaves of autumn hues, sunflowers, pumpkins and gourds. The most amazing thing, I believe, is how this miraculous milestone of earth and time passes almost unnoticed by the mundane multitudes.

My Celebration

I welcome the growing darkness that I know will follow Mabon. Moment by moment, day by day, it creeps up almost unnoticed. Until one day, you glance at the clock and realize that afternoon is barely over, evening has barely begun, and it is pitch dark outside.

My favorite way to celebrate Mabon is by lighting candles all over the house. In doing so I'm actually celebrating the darkness with light.

I light white candles for cleansing and purification, for Spirit, for the Goddess. I light white candles to wipe the slate clean, to start new lists, to begin new projects. I light yellow candles to celebrate the sun and its grace and dignity as it steps back to make way for the moon. I light yellow candles to celebrate communication and everything I've ever wanted to say to anyone, and those things I might regret not saying. I light yellow candles to fill my mind with words and thoughts that run into sentences and paragraphs and pages. I light lavender candles to celebrate the spirits I know are there, but cannot see. I light lavender candles to acknowledge that little voice in my head, the one that's saved my life over the years, not to mention my sanity. I light green candles to celebrate and embrace the earth. I light green candles to celebrate and embrace this wonderful physical body that is mine. I light green candles to bathe in the glow of good health and prosperity. I light green candles to feel the soles of my bare feet connect with the dying grass, the withering garden, the falling leaves.

I light one tall black taper candle that is me, to celebrate the spark of life I carry, to celebrate future days to come, to celebrate my passage through another year... and to acknowledge and embrace my mortality.

Mabon Correspondences

Herbs: Marigold, myrrh, thistles, sage

Altar Flowers/Herbs: Asters, mums, pine, ferns, milkweed, honey-suckle

Feast Foods: Autumn berries, nuts, roast game, root vegetables, cider, wine, bread

Animals: Stags, goats, blackbirds, canines, owls, birds-of-prey

Incense: Cedar, myrrh, patchouli, pine, sage, sweet grass, oak moss

Rituals/Spells: Drying herbs, gathering late harvest, past life work, harvest moon rituals, making willow wands, harmony spells, protection spells for winter

Mabon Recipes

Caramel Apple Crumb Treat
Ingredients:
2 Golden Delicious apples
4 small (or 2 large) Granny Smith apples
⅛ cup fruit juice
⅓ cup loosely packed light brown sugar
2 tablespoons butter
¼ teaspoon ground ginger
12 soft caramel candies
½ cup quick rolled oats
½ cup flour
⅓ cup tightly packed light brown sugar
½ teaspoon ground ginger
⅓ cup butter

Slice and core the apples, mixing the types together.

Pour the fruit juice into a large pot. Put about a third of the apple slices into the pot. Sprinkle with half the lightly packed brown sugar and dot with 1 tablespoon of butter. Add more apples and the remaining brown sugar and butter, and ¼ teaspoon ground ginger.

Turn the heat on low and simmer for a while. Stir the apples occasionally, until they start to soften. The Golden Delicious will pretty much turn to mush, binding together the slices of Granny Smith. This takes about an hour or two, depending on the heat and the apples.

Meanwhile, cut the soft caramels into quarters.

Preheat the oven to 350 degrees F.

To prepare the crumble topping, stir together ½ cup quick rolled oats, ½ cup flour, ⅓ cup tightly packed light brown sugar, and ½ teaspoon ground ginger. Slice ⅓ cup butter and add to the bowl, then cut it in with a butter cutter until the mixture is loose and crumbly.

Spray a ceramic or glass pie plate with cooking spray. Spoon in about a third of the apples and spread them on the bottom. Top with half the caramel pieces. Spoon in another third of the apples; top with the remaining caramel pieces. Spoon in the remaining apples and spread them smooth. Use another spoon to sprinkle the crumble topping evenly over the top of the apple filling.

Bake for 20-30 minutes until the filling is bubbly and the topping melds into a lightly golden crust. Serve hot.

Broccoli Casserole

Ingredients:

2 eggs, lightly beaten

1 can (10 ¾ ounces) condensed cream of mushroom soup, undiluted

1 medium onion, chopped

1 cup (4 ounces) shredded cheddar cheese

1 cup (4 ounces) shredded Swiss cheese

½ cup mayonnaise

2 tablespoons butter, melted

1 package (16 ounces) frozen broccoli cuts, thawed

1 package (10 ounces) frozen chopped broccoli, thawed

¼ cup dry breadcrumbs

In a large bowl, combine the first seven ingredients; fold in the broccoli. Transfer to a greased 1½ qt. baking dish. Sprinkle with breadcrumbs. Cover and bake at 400 degrees F for 30-35 minutes or until heated through. Serves 8.

Part 5

A Woman's Life Transitions

Maiden, Mother and Crone

Maiden

I suddenly come alive within my body in wonder and acknowledgment of its miracle. I feel it as I am, it is, I am... I am... I am, I keep telling myself in amazement. I'm here, on the inside, looking out, listening, learning, watching, absorbing. No one knows this, the people around me seem unaware of it, the world seems unaware of it, but it's true. I wave my hands wildly, my spirit trying desperately to be acknowledged, to be recognized. I'm like a sponge ready to absorb all that life has to offer me, all that I can grasp with eager hands, an eager soul, an eager body, an eager mind. What will I feel? What will I learn? How will I grow? How do I begin this journey in earnest, really, how do I push off and begin to move forward? And how will I know when I've reached my destination?

Color for the Maiden: White
Moon Phase: Waxing
Her Influence: New beginnings

Mother

They all turn to me – the children, the husband, the community, the world. I am the center of the wheel. The universe is spinning around me as I create, build, grow, come alive with new ideas, and immerse myself in new projects. The spokes of the wheel come to me, racing through space and time from all directions, and me solitary and still at the center, taking the blows of life full-force. I am in the middle of life, going at a hundred miles an hour, watching the world around me race by in a blur of color and shapes. This is my time, my time to succeed, my time to taste the glory of life, my time to fill all the empty spaces. I feel that all the world, all the wild things in it, all the green things in it, are growing from something within the center of me. I was, I am, I will be. How can I keep from being absorbed by all the frenetic scattered energy and activity around me? How can I maintain my own identity without losing it amongst the myriad roles that I play in this life?

Color for the Mother: Red
Moon Phase: Full
Her Influence: Ongoing projects, birth

Crone

Sometimes I'm tired, tired of the physical struggles of life. I'm tired of cleaning this house, I'm tired of trying to pull everything together for everyone around me. I'm tired of carrying life's responsibilities on my shoulders for so long, through so much, through good times and through crises. I'm tired; I'm old and I'm tired. I would just like to sit in a chair, beneath a tree, with my hand on a cat and listen... listen to the wind in the leaves, listen to the earth beneath my feet, listen to the cat beneath my hand, listen to the birds and voice of nature. I want to be still, if even for a moment, and listen to the whisper in my ear, the voice of the Goddess. She's calling to me now, her voice laced with a sense of urgency. She's waiting for my answer. Have I learned enough? Have I done enough? Have I finished my tasks? What is left to do?

Color for the Crone: Black
Moon Phase: Waning
Her Influence: Death and rebirth

Making and Breaking Divine Connections

Learn to recognize what it is about you, in you, and around you that allows you to connect with the Divine. But it's just as important for you to learn what it is about you, in you, and around you that **breaks** this connection. *"Learn to control your mind,"* my spirit guide whispered in my ear many years ago. In other words, learn to control your thoughts, learn to channel positive energy. But, at the same time, you also have to learn to recognize negative thoughts and emotions and feelings, learn to harness this, to stop it, to avert it.

You need to recognize what connects you to The Divine, and you need to recognize what breaks this connection.

You *are* what you feel and think and imagine; your life *is* what you think and feel and imagine. You can draw in positive energy and people and circumstances, or you can draw in the negative aspect of all these things. What are you feeling right now? Happy? Sad? If you feel sad, what's making you feel this way? What could you think of, what thought could you pop into your head right now, this very minute, to change the sad emotion into a positive emotion?

The secret is that **You** are in control.

This energy creates a divine connection:

1. Mental clarity
2. Good physical health
3. Love
4. Understanding
5. Generosity
6. Benevolence
7. Happiness
8. Self-confidence

9. Sacrifice (as in being able to put someone else, or a cause, first)
10. Modesty (defined as a humble sort of energy)

This energy breaks the divine connection:

1. Substance abuse
2. Illness
3. Hate
4. Misunderstanding
5. Envy
6. Jealousy
7. Abuse
8. Bigotry
9. Arrogance
10. Conceit

Meditate, concentrate, become aware, know your own mind. Recognize the flow of both positive and negative energy and thoughts. Learn to "change channels", to switch gears, in midstream. Learn to manipulate your thoughts as well as your emotions to produce positive life circumstances.

Like attracts like... the thoughts you are thinking, the feelings you experience, the expectations you have, all of these things will predetermine what your day will be like – what your life will be like! It's all magick, all of it; it's nothing more or less than manipulating energy, moving energy to create change. What kind of change depends on what kind of energy you're moving.

Just like Tinker Bell teaching the Darling children to fly: "You have to think a happy thought!"

Think positive thoughts... and soar!

Remember... You are in control.

Part 6

Turning Mundane Milestones into Spiritual Rituals

First Menstruation

Do you remember the first day of your menstruation? I do, and I think most women have this day seared in their memory. It was the day that we left childhood behind and became something magickal and remarkable... *women*.

From the moment that I first learned about menstruation through a fifth grade class film, I looked forward to this momentous experience, this amazing and beautiful transition. I was prepared for it, I was impatient for it, I was awed by it, and I welcomed it, and all that came with it – the discomfort, the inconvenience, but it didn't matter. All that mattered was the miracle my body had become.

It's a sad fact that our culture, our western society, tends to be very secretive about this topic in general, and a girl's first menstruation in particular. It's all hush-hush, like some dirty little secret best kept under wraps. How awful that we make our girl-children self-conscious and maybe even ashamed of such a stupendous event, a once-in-a-life time "first".

So let's change this. Let's celebrate a girl's entrance into womanhood with congratulations, cheer, laughter, and merriment. Whether it be your daughter, granddaughter, or niece, prepare a celebration to mark this first major milestone in her young life.

Ritual Suggestions

First, let's establish that this celebration is for women only. It's our moment, it's all about the feminine perspective. It's a celebration given by women for a new young woman. Those gathering should be female friends and relatives.

The moon phase will be the full to waxing moon; and it would be delightful if the young woman's first period coincided with this phase of the moon, but if it not, you can improvise. Either plan the celebration around the actual date of first menstruation, or plan the celebration around the appropriate moon phase, or the full moon following this event.

How do we decorate the table for a First Menstruation Celebration?

One way is to choose one of the goddesses who will be invoked and honored during this celebration, and in this case, I'm going to choose the Maiden goddess Artemis. This celebration will actually be bidding her, and this first phase of life, good bye. We're going to use candle colors, herbs, and such that align with Artemis to honor the Maiden aspect this young woman is leaving behind, emphasizing that each magickal phase of a woman's life gives her an opportunity to learn and to grow into the mature woman she is meant to be, and each phase moves along naturally, according to nature, transitioning smoothly.

The table will be decorated with a white lace cloth, pretty and feminine. The flowers will be pink primroses; the candles will be green and white and red; the incense will be patchouli.

Fill the table with favorite goodies and sweet treats. Keep everything casual, light-hearted, and fun. But at some point during this celebration, the young woman and her mother, or a chosen female friend representing the Mother aspect, should stand together at the table and in unison, their hands joined, extinguish the white candle and light a red pillar candle in honor of the occasion. This is representative of the Mother welcoming the Maiden; it's representative of a girl's transition from childhood to womanhood. By extinguishing the white candle, we bid adieu to one phase of life and set out on a path that will lead to another. Other women gathered at the celebration can come forward to hug, kiss, and congratulate the young lady on her passage, perhaps giving her presents (a significant pendent necklace, perhaps), flowers, and such.

Oh! Joy! I am the woman I dreamed of being!

The most important thing is that this milestone, this awesome all important event in a girl's life is celebrated and acknowledged.

Childbirth

Your life will never be the same after the birth of your first child. You are no longer the center of your world... your child is. Becoming a mother is perhaps the most profound life-altering event a woman will ever experience. It is awe-inspiring. When this brand new individual is born, you're going to spend many happy hours staring into their little face, admiring their sweet baby tush and tiny toes, and marveling that someday this wee bundle of squirming squealing humanity is going to grow up to be something marvelous – a mature adult.

Ritual/Celebration Suggestions

Red: Symbolic of the Mother; symbolic of menstruation; symbolic of birth.

Celebrate with: Red flowers; red gifts, whether pretty nighties or sweaters, or bottled perfumes; candles; good things to eat (apples!); jewelry and stones (garnets and rubies!); statues and baubles; shawls; goblets, or wine... **Red.**

I've heard of an ancient American Native custom of burying the placenta in the earth and planting a tree above it. I love this, not only because trees are dear to me and I have an ongoing love affair with them, but because the whole idea of continued growth and continuity is so linked to birth and to trees.

On this child's 18th birthday, he/she can stand beneath this tree and absorb through the earth its energy, the love that went into its planting, and the universal wisdom and knowledge that naturally flow through the sacred roots and stems and branches of *their Birth Tree*.

Menopause

There is a combination of emotions centered around this event in a woman's life; and this is an ongoing transition, remember. If a natural menopause is experienced, you will not wake up some morning to abruptly find yourself transitioned from Mother to Crone. It doesn't work that way. This too, this last phase of woman's life, it is still a learning process, a gradual awakening. And yes, it's an awakening, it's not an end. Menopause is simply another beginning, a new beginning. You will be allowed now to view the world, your life and the divine, from a whole new perspective.

You will come full circle; you will taste the victory of having lived and learned, of having lived and survived, of having lived to reach the stage you are now, the most illuminating and beautiful stage of a woman's life. This is your time. Finally, after years of being someone's daughter, someone's wife, someone's mother, someone's grandmother, it's time to re-center. It's time to refocus, it's time to renew a relationship with yourself.

Personal Menopause Rituals

Things You Want To Leave Behind

List all of these things on a single piece of paper, whether they are actual physical things or people, or whether they are circumstances, emotions, and such that have been bothering you. You can list them all on one great big piece of paper because they are one great big lump of crap that needs to be disposed of. And this is exactly what you're going to do; you're going to dispose of this list and these negative things, people, and circumstances by putting this paper in a box, a small cardboard box, the kind that you will find in a hobby/craft shop, those little ones that are just waiting to be decorated.

How do you want to get rid of it?

If you bury it in the earth – off your property and a distance away! – these things will most certainly stop bothering you, but they may not go completely away. They will still be there, but the feeling of them will be sort of blunt, a far-off: "Oh, ya, I remember_____ , funny how I haven't thought of that in a while."

This might be okay if what you want to rid yourself of is something that you might want to change, but not necessarily banish completely from your life.

For things that you really truly want to go completely away, never to come back, take this little box and find a nice rushing stream, or a river, a body of water with a flow to it, not a stagnant pool or lake. Stop on a bridge, or take a nice walk along the bank, and when you're ready, throw this box in the moving water. Sling it out there, give it some oomph. After all, this is stuff you want as far away from you as possible. Be sure to show the universe just how strongly you feel about it. (If you happen to stomp your feet, or throw a few cuss words out there, or spit – that's okay, you're making your point.)

Things You Still Want To Accomplish

This sounds like a "Bucket List", but it's more than that. This isn't just Things-You-Wish-You-Could-Do-Before-You-Die. These are actual things that you were put here to do. They are things you were meant to do. They are things that just got postponed while you were busy having babies, raising a family, earning a wage, and taking care of all the things Life threw your way and made your responsibility.

Now it's your turn.

What do you still want to accomplish? What do you have left to do?

Make a list. Sit on a quiet day, over a cup of coffee, looking out a rainy window, and think of all of the wonderful, incredible, simple, complicated, difficult, and easy things that you still want to do. Write this list on a plain piece of paper, or on a paper laced with flowers, or on a paper with stars in the background, or on a paper with no lines or boundaries at all.

Get a small box for this piece of paper too. The ones I spoke of, those small boxes that are just waiting to be decorated. You're going to keep this one, and you might even decorate it – decorate it with wishes and fantasies, dreams and realities. You're going to keep it close by, handy enough so that you can open it every now and then and look at this list, and check things off as you get them done, and add new things to the bottom of the list to do, because you are not stagnant, but incredibly creative and adventurous.

This is your I-Am-An-Amazing-Woman-Box.

Birthdays

Another year passes. With the first birthdays, in the Maiden stage, each one becomes a celebratory milestone, but after a woman reaches 30 in our culture, we begin to associate a feeling of trepidation with the passing of another year. Why? What's not to celebrate? Forget that our society foolishly worships youth and suffers from a chronic case of Peter Pan syndrome; instead, celebrate, be joyful, embrace each year, embrace each change within yourself. *You are not aging, you are growing.* This is the difference, this is what our culture, our society, doesn't see, or tries to deny. With time women grow wiser, more assertive, more complete within themselves. *They bloom!*

Grow, Sweet Woman, grow in time, grow in wisdom, grow in laughter, grow in strength, grow in love, grow in power, grow in creativity, grow in magick.

Excel.

Succeed.

Experience.

Enjoy.

The 10th Year[3]
The Threshold: Childhood to Maidenhood
I still have one foot in the world of my childhood, but I can see through the open threshold before me. The view is hazy yet. It's still so early, and I am still so young. I see a shadow of the woman I will become.

The 20th Year
The Threshold: Adolescence to Adulthood
I'm taking baby steps, trying out my adult legs, finding my center. Which direction will I go? Where will I establish my roots? The roots of career and relationships. The foundation I

build now will determine the stability of my future. Is it really all just a roll of the dice, or does destiny lie in my young and inexperienced hands?

The 30th Year
The Threshold: Maidenhood to Motherhood
I step through a doorway to find myself standing in the mad rush of Life. I am careening along at full speed, swerving to avoid potholes, watching the clock, knowing that I have a destination and a dead line to meet, knowing I have an appointment with Responsibility.

The 40th Year
The Threshold: Motherhood to Middle Age
I'm at a crossroads, no longer young, but not yet old. The world around me appears to lose focus as boundaries and expectations are blurred. What once was perfectly clear is now laced with questions. The Universe is giving me a choice. I watch in alarmed fascination as new paths open before me, each yellow brick road beckoning me, "Come this way!"

The 50th Year
The Threshold: Middle Age to Crone
I suddenly realize who I am, I mean the "me" that I must have lost along the way. I suddenly realize that the only opinion that counts is my own. I suddenly realize who my friends are and who they aren't. I suddenly realize that I am not afraid to face the world alone. I suddenly realize that I have reached a plateau enabling me to scrutinize my past and glimpse my future. I suddenly realize... I have arrived.

The 60th Year
The Threshold: The Crone to the Golden Age
I'm at a crossroads, no longer middle-aged, but not yet old, not

really, I say with defiance. My body speaks to me now, still proud of its strength, its endurance. My body speaks to me with relish, embracing the last blazing autumn of life.

The 70th Year

The Threshold: The Golden Age to Old Age

I will reap what I have sown, whether this be children, grandchildren, great-grandchildren, or the golden glow of accomplishments. I will stop to smell the roses. I will stop to watch the sunset. I will stop to pet a dog, or hold a cat. I will stop to speak to an old friend. I will stop to say, "I love you;" "Hello;" "Goodbye;" and "I'm sorry."

The 80th Year

The Threshold: The Crone Glorified

I am elevated. From this vantage point I stand in the stillness of dawn. I stand in the midst of gentle rain on black earth. I stand in the warmth of a loved one's hand on my arm. I stand, not in the shadow of the Crone, but shoulder to shoulder with her. I am one with the Goddess.

The 90th Year

The Threshold: Rebirth

I look at the world and see it as hazy images in a crystal ball. The images are people I've loved, places I've been, things I've done. And as I stare at the images within this universal sphere, I can see that they are fading, getting dimmer, and soon they will disappear. I know that as these images and this world are fading. I know there is another beautiful glorious crystal ball, and within it I can see the sunrise bursting over the horizon, lighting the way for a new journey... in the next Life.

Wedding Showers

We celebrate the fact that one becomes two. We celebrate the success of finding a mate. Yes, we do, even though most feminists might flinch at this. She did good, they'll say, eye-balling the future husband, holding him up to their personal measuring stick. But this is not only the celebration of a coupling, it's celebrating the creation of a new family. As the future bride opens her pretty packaged gifts, this will be evident amongst all the shiny new pots and pans, the toaster, and the coffee-maker. This young woman and her fiancé will be setting up house, preparing for a lifetime together to build memories, to raise children, to grow old together. In our modern world, as progressive and feminist as we'd like to think we are, we're still chasing Prince Charming and Happy-Ever-After endings.

Creating the Home = Creating Sacred Space

The Kitchen
For most families, this is the center of the home, the hearthfire, where the group gathers for sustenance, for company, for recreation, for connection. I don't know about everyone else, but anything that goes down in our house goes down in the kitchen. Our large kitchen table doubles as my office, the classroom, the dining table, the game board, card table, and craft table. Things are written, sculpted, painted, eaten, played, and produced – all at the kitchen table.

The kitchen is the hub, and shower gifts for this room, this special space, are prolific and fun to buy and give. I've been married five times and I've never had a wedding shower, so I'm living vicariously here in this section, remembering (with a wee bit of envy, I admit) all of the cool things new brides can receive to set up their hearthfire. But there's one big difference here, we're going to look at all of these gifts from a magickal and spiritual perspective. We're going to wallow in Bridal Mania and Goddess Energy.

Herbs

One of the coolest gifts I've seen was a huge beautiful wooden shelf full of bottles and bottles of herbs, large glass bottles. The Green Witch in me was twitching! The wooden cubby-holed rack was dark cherry wood, and the whole frame swiveled, so you could turn it, looking at four sides full of glass bottles full of wonderful magickal plants and spices. However, as grand and glorious as this was, this wonderful gift does not have to break our piggy bank. Herbs are expensive, and they are so uniquely necessary, both mundanely and magickally, for cooking and witchy revelry.

If everyone is counting their pennies, but you still want the new bride to start out with a well-stocked herb cabinet, each guest can bring one designated herb. Co-ordinate this so that each individual knows exactly what to purchase – Aunt Lacey is in charge of parsley; Cousin Edie is going to be responsible for rosemary; Grandma Betty is bringing cardamom, etc., etc.

Oh Green Witch rejoice!

Pots and Pans

Oh my, this sounds so dreary, bringing to mind the scullery maid chained to the kitchen peeling potatoes, wiping sweat from her brow with her brown work-worn paw... Screeeech! (The tape rewinds.)

Pots and pans, think about it... drum roll... **The Cauldron!**

This is where all our magick brews, it is the myth of the witch, it is Shakespearian and dramatic, highly visual, slightly daunting to the uninitiated individuals, and highly gratifying to the Witches Extraordinaire.

Mundane Pots and Pans: You know, those Teflon pots are nice for a while, but it's really a drag when the Teflon gets scratched and then begins to peel and flake; and if you're like I am, having come from a humble background, you don't just toss it out when the first few worn marks and flaws show up. If you're anything like me, you use it until it is disgusting and two or three kids have attempted to throw it out and finally hidden it so deeply within the depths of the trash that you won't find it. So, if money is an issue, but not that much of an issue, my suggestion would be stainless steel. Stainless steel pots and pans will last forever.

Magickal Pots and Pans: This part is much more fun. I'm thinking... special pots for specific magickal workings. I'm thinking color-co-ordinated cooking pots, those pretty bright enamel (and usually Teflon-lined) pots. I know, this is an irony, but this is special! It's for magickal workings, energy building and moving and shaking. It's all about getting things done.

A green pot could be for health and healing, for simmering teas and making infusions, all the while tossing in the energy to fix whatever is wrong with our physical, emotional, and mental selves. (You have to look at it from all those perspectives, it's all wrapped up into us.) You can use this pot to mix and heat magickal oils as well, but one word of caution here; if you're going to be using these pots for teas and such that you ingest, don't use them for other magickal creations that would contain anything poisonous or dangerous.

The rest is easy. A red pot for love and lust and passion; blue for dreams and visions, psychism, and divination; yellow for creativity and communication; and if you think you might venture into deeper waters and work with darker energies, or anything that is stronger and not meant to be ingested, why don't you get a small silver or black pot for this.

The Stove
This is the modern version of the hearthfire, use your imagination for the crackling flames and the dancing shadows on the

wall. I also have a wonderful gift idea for the new bride and her stove. Think of the flame (the burners) as you would a flame in a cauldron. When you've finished your magickal workings, you generally dismiss the quarters and the elements. To put the magick to rest, you can have a set of those round metal burner covers made and decorated with the symbols for the elements – Earth, Air, Water, Fire. The symbolism and the artistry that could go into them are endless, whether you want to keep it simple and just use the correct color symbol for that element, or really go to town... birds and flying creature on the cover for Air; the sea, sea creatures, and sea shells on the cover for Water... you get the point.

The Living Room
Think of gifts geared for relaxation, for reading, for communication, as this is often a lounging and gathering place for family members. Think of things to write with; board games; books; big soft pillows and pretty small blankets for the couch or easy chair; candy dishes for the end tables or coffee table; a tea set that comes with a serving tray. I can see all of these delightful things in my mind, and I can see the space that they're meant for being cozy and inviting, where you feel comfortable and relaxed.

The idea of communication and creativity come to me when I think of a living room space, which steers me towards CDs, books, DVDs (movies! Yay!)... something to watch, listen to, or read.

The living room, think serenity and peace, think communication and connection.

The Bathroom
The Element: Water
The Main Intent and Purpose in this Room: Cleansing!
Did you ever wonder why, in so many bathrooms you see, people just naturally tend to decorate with sea themes, sea and

water creatures, sea shells and other things of the ocean or water-related? I really believe it's some ingrained instinct, not fashionable decorating fads, that leads them to these water-based interior designs for the bathroom.

So, we got the water creatures and stuff down pat, but there are other things to think about that would make incredible and magickal shower gifts for the bathroom:

Bowls

Large glass bowls or lidded containers filled with herbs aligned to the element of Water – belladonna, catnip, calamus, cardamom, henbane, valerian, raspberry, rose, myrrh, passion flower, and on and on it goes (pick up Scott Cunningham's book, *Encyclopedia of Magickal Herbs* or *A Kitchen Witch's World of Magical Herbs & Plants* by Rachel Patterson, published by Moon Books). While we're at it, what about live potted plants for the bathroom? I'd love live plants for shower gifts, and I'm betting other women would too – roses, jasmine, gardenias, or African violets, all connected with the element of Water.

Candles

So obvious! When you fill the tub with nice hot water, topping it off with a handful of herbs and pinch of this or that with a dollop of bubbly stuff, you're going to light candles to set the mood for your bathing experience. *Ding*...that was the light bulb going off in my head! It's saying, "Time to shop!" How fun to look for candles and candle holders for someone's bathroom; and it might be a good idea to play heavily on the personal likes and tastes of the new bride you're buying these magickal gifts for. Candle holders will add so much to the personal aspect of it, pick holders in different styles, colors, and shapes (animals, leaves, and such). Have fun! Shop till you drop, then go home and run yourself a nice full tub of water and prepare to relax.

The Bedroom

Oh my, this is the supreme sacred space, especially for the newly-wed couple; and I don't care if they've been sleeping together for years. The wedding night is going to be so magickal, this is extremely special. This space will seem somehow newly sanctified to them through a commitment ceremony. It will be sealed. It will be celebrated.

The elements? The energy?

This space is a bit conflicted on this point. There's actually two elements that will apply to this room and two very different types of energy. We'll look at both of them.

1. *Fire:* Passion, lust, romantic love, all of which implies lots of energy; lots of physicality; lots of motion and a sharing of energies. This can be wonderful, but also exhausting.
2. *Water:* Peace, dreams, visions, of course. This is where you sleep, where your body renews itself, where your mind relaxes, where your sub-conscious can take over and you can soar in your dreams.

What a wonderful, yet complicated, space to create. Depending upon the couple and their circumstances, you might want magickal gifts geared to fertility and sex. At the other end of the spectrum, you'll want gifts that add to the experience of relaxation and peace. I know, this room is an oxymoron, and it can get even more confusing if the energies of the two individuals who are inhabiting this space are conflicting, or even polar opposites.

For the wedding shower, offer up a bit of magickal energy and a touch of the Goddess through crystals and stones; salt lamps; candles; herbs; mojo bags for protection, fertility, cleansing; statuary that inspires, inspirational CD/DVDs that will add a certain ambiance to the atmosphere.

Baby Showers

Baby showers... the ultimate complete all-out joyful celebration of a future life. But it's also a personal celebration as a young woman stands on the threshold of motherhood, entering a daunting, rewarding, often exhausting, and ultimately magickal time of life. As we help this woman prepare for the physical needs of the new baby, we are girding up her loins, letting her know that there are mothers, grandmothers, aunts, sisters, and friends among her circle who will offer a helping hand with this task, whether it be a bit of advice when needed, or actual physical help with all the duties that go along with having a baby, running a home, and raising children.

They say, "It takes a village," and, in a way, it does. It's nice to know that we have a group of women in our lives who we can depend upon for support.

Now, for the Baby Shower itself:

Remember the fairy tale of Sleeping Beauty? The parents of the little princess invited the forest fairies (or witches, whatever they were), and each magickal guest endowed the child with a very special gift, an attribute or a blessing. You can do the same thing for your own Magickal Baby Shower. You'll have people who will bring conventional, mundane gifts, and people who will bring magickal gifts, and people who will do both.

If you are a guest for just such a shower, you can package your magickal gift so it is as beautiful and memorable as any of the other gifts presented.

Candle
Make a special candle for the baby (blue or pink is traditional and cute, or choose another pastel color if you prefer to avoid gender stereotypes). Carve the appropriate sigils into the candle, as well as baby's name, if it's known, to go along with your intention and

the magickal energy you are passing on to this lucky infant. Decorate the candle. And you can go hog wild here with sparkles and ribbons; or glue on cute pins, buttons, flower blossoms; mix and match up beadwork and paint; modgepodge photos or other images. The ideas are endless, and if you're really stuck for an idea, there's always Pinterest!

Scroll

You can decorate with sparkles and ribbon, and some rocking calligraphy, a scroll with your magickal wishes written upon it, tied up with a blue, pink or other pastel colored ribbon.

Witch's Bottle

You can create a witch's bottle for the baby, with all kinds of cool things in it related to your particular magickal gift, including herbs, flower blossoms, coins, stones, crystals and such. This would really be a beautiful keepsake, and your magickal intention amplified with the bottle, the colors, textures, and other items used. It could actually be something the child might have forever, a permanent reminder that someone cared so much about their arrival into this world that they bestowed upon them magick!

Part 7

Finding the Goddess in Tarot

Motherpeace Tarot:
A Personal and Uniquely Feminine Journey

Tarot is what I do. It is an integral part of my life and my journey with the Goddess. My journey through the landscape of the feminine divine would not be complete if I didn't travel this path with a deck of tarot cards in my hand. The deck, Motherpeace, was perfect for this journey. When viewing and interpreting these cards, I made sure I was "zenned-out", in the frame of mind to view each image through the eyes of Woman, through the eyes of my sisters, my feminine ancestors, and the Goddess. It was almost as if she were speaking to me, and it is with great pleasure and anticipation that I pass on to you the wisdom whispered in my ear.

The Major Arcana of the tarot deck are most often referred to as the cards of "Fate". These cards will force you to face that which you've been denying, avoiding, or trying to hide, either from yourself or others. They are Life's Lessons 101, with no opportunity to cram for the exam. At a deeper level, when used for personal meditation and introspection, these cards will open the deepest recesses of your subconscious, revealing the lush world of color beneath the mundane and ordinary surface, much as when Dorothy opened the door of her black-and-white world to reveal the Technicolor of Oz.

Major Arcana

0 Fool

The character on this card is doing handsprings along a running stream, surrounded by a vulture, a cat, and an alligator. At the end of the stream, right in the midst of it, stands a blossoming lotus. This card tells us not to be afraid of the future, to live life with gusto and joy. A satchel is balanced on her foot, along with a peacock's feather, reminding us to take with us into life all that we need, be prepared, and hold tight to a sense of high self-esteem. You're not alone, the Fool tells us. Although in essence everyone's journey through life is solitary, it's punctuated and altered by all those we meet and those who touch our lives, if even for the briefest moment. Discern who are your friends and who would wish you ill. Keep your eyes open on this journey, but don't let fear or indecision stand in your way.

1 Magician

Stealth, illusion, power, and mystery are encased within the figure on this card, a female figure wearing the skin of a leopard. *"You shall see what I wish you to see,"* says this mistress of magick. The four elements are held in the palm of her hand and directed by her will: the passion of Fire, the visions of Water, the wisdom of Air, and the balance of Earth. They rule, and she rules them, teaching us that the power is ours, hidden within ancient ancestral memories, buried beneath centuries of oppression, it has been set free… and so have we.

2 High Priestess

She encompasses Woman at her most base level, and you'd think she wouldn't, but she does. The High Priestess should be all spiritual and above the physical world, but she isn't; it's all entwined together for us, for women. Each new physical experience, from first menstruation, to sexual awakening, to childbirth, elevates us to a new spiritual level. It is the way of woman. The squatting primitive figure on this card, sitting with open outstretched hands and spread legs, is drawing into herself wisdom from the past, from her sisters, from her ancestors, from feminine divinity. She is imbued with power and inner strength. She's open to the energy. That's what this card is all about, being open to the energy.

3 Empress

This card is wide hips and breasts full of milk, knowledge, history, and strength. It reaches into the past, far beyond the clutches of Christianity, to a deeper time when we were more connected to the earth and nature's natural cycles. It dances the joyful dance of femininity, the dance of the wise-woman. The Empress luxuriates in all that is hidden and cloistered within our subconscious. She is our base raw sexuality. She is the essence of the witch, the female shaman, the matriarch in all her old glory. Through her lineage all women are connected, and one day the world will turn once more to the Divine Matriarch and set destiny upon an old new path.

4 Emperor

This card is all about male energy, so how can we incorporate this card on a spiritually feminist journey? Easy, this card is all about accepting the stronger aspects of your personality. It's about embracing the masculine side of yourself, learning to grow with it, learning to run with it, learning to configure this energy into your daily life when necessary. So many women shy away from this side of themselves, perhaps because it goes against what they feel is expected from them as females – to be all soft and nurturing, forgiving, loving, and gentle. The Emperor helps us embrace the idea that sometimes we will be dealing with people, or situations, in life where we will need to draw on the masculine side of ourselves to be gritty, to be strong, and even ruthless.

5 Hierophant

Spirituality; this is the card that speaks of spirituality. In traditional decks it is stamped with "conformity", but not here, not in the Motherpeace tarot. From the bare-breasted priestess with arms extended and palms raised sky-ward, to the scrolls and other religious symbols portrayed among a group of women, the energy on this card completely envelops our spiritual side. It acknowledges the varied spiritual paths available to us. It acknowledges the fact that each individual must follow the spiritual path that feels right for them, and it acknowledges the fact that many of us will spend a lifetime (or several lifetimes) experimenting before we find our way. The male figure in the background, a sword in both hands raised in reverence and worship, reminds us that the Goddess is also mother to our fathers, husbands, brothers, and sons. Help the men in your life embrace the feminine divine.

6 Lovers

More than physical love and passion, this card is about "balance" and the spiritual connection between two souls. The yin/yang principle is illustrated with two abstract figures that highlight the center of the card, and this theme of duality is carried throughout with other images. The Lovers card in Motherpeace reminds us that in order to achieve a real connection with someone, which involves focusing on all that encompasses human development – emotional, mental, *and* physical aspects, we often have to overcome obstacles and build a relationship one stone at a time, from the ground up. It's this type of foundation that lends itself to magickal connections that last a lifetime.

7 Chariot

With freedom comes movement, with movement comes choices, with choices comes decisions, with decisions comes responsibility. The Chariot is telling us that in the end we are responsible for plotting our own course, for turning the direction of our lives around, for making changes within the arena of daily living that sweeps us to new levels of awareness. And the Chariot of the Motherpeace deck reminds us that, as women, the movement we precipitate affects not only us, but all those around us, the bystanders – children, mates, friends, and family. Freedom may ring loudly and boisterously, but in the background responsibility sits quietly and heavily, riding upon our coat tails, even as we run barefoot through the meadow, pretending we are completely carefree.

8 Justice

There are three figures on this card, one with her hand on a horned stag (truth and justice through the God), one holding her hand in the running water of a falls (truth and justice through the Goddess), and one seated beneath a tree holding a turtle (truth and justice will come with time, you can't rush the process). And so it is. This card tells us that instant revenge, instant retaliation, are not always wise, and in fact are the wrong way to view a situation, or to deal with life's issues. As the three figures on this card wait and watch, with patience and fortitude, they know that the universe will right a wrong. They know that justice will prevail, just not as we humans might envision it.

9 Crone

The Crone emphasizes that this phase of a woman's life isn't a culmination or a climax, it's a journey. It's everything in-between that it took to get to this point in your life. On the card in the Motherpeace tarot, the wise old Crone in the forefront is looking back, perhaps with a hint of wistfulness and a sense of appreciation to the two figures behind her representing the Maiden and the Mother. You see, you can't get to where you're going without acknowledging where you've been. But make no mistake about it, this card highlights the wisdom you gleaned along the way. It highlights the round of applause you deserve for getting through life, and getting through it in spite of adversity, doubt, self-deception, and self-sabotage.

10 Wheel of Fortune

This card tells us that energies are aligned; accomplishments will be celebrated. The center of this card shows planets aligned all in a row, and this is how our life will come to be ordered when the Wheel of Fortune shows its face. The characters around the edge of this card are ancient magickal archetypes for the feminine in all shapes and forms, attitudes and traditions. This card challenges us to view ourselves in sheer undistorted honesty. This card challenges us to accept ourselves in all our shapes, and forms, and stages of life. This card says bluntly, "I am what I am."

11 Strength

Through woman all living things find comfort, healing, warmth, and sustenance. The touch of the Goddess has created this world, and it is her spirit that sustains all life and assures its continuity. It is the nurturing aspect of woman that is honored and emphasized on this card. The picture shows a woman sitting naked in a field of green as animals of all kinds come to her, to be renewed and strengthened by the touch of her hand by the power of her magickal energy. And it is this archetype that is embraced within this Major Arcana card, to be passed on to us, that we may embrace this strength also, that it shall become part of us.

12 Hanged One

The Hanged One is an analogy of woman's life. Its most important acknowledgment is self-sacrifice; and then illumination and revelation through self-analysis; spiritual enlightenment through solitary meditation and magickal practice; and self-discovery. It also represents a suspension of time, a suspension of forward movement, the idea of being forced to come to a standstill and listen, listen to our inner voice, to the divine that's trying to connect deep within our psyche. Listen to our ancestors; to our sisters; and most importantly, listen to ourselves – our real selves, not the image we show to the world. When we learn all we were meant to learn, only then will we be freed from the tether, to plant our feet firmly once more on Mother Earth.

13 Death

On this card skeletal remains lie at the base of a white birch tree surrounded by a fluttering of golden autumn leaves and a snake. This card speaks of transitions, of natural stages opening and closing, one into the other. It speaks of wisdom and spirituality following us on our journey through this life and afterward. It speaks of a time to rest and retreat from earthly concerns, a time to go inward, reaching to a deepness we may never have attempted before, or a place inside ourselves where we may have been afraid to go.

14 Temperance

Unlike the traditional image of Temperance on other decks, the figure on this card is a far cry from the staid angel. The female figure on this card is a bare-chested grass-skirted wild woman, shaking her body, shouting affirmations and proclamations, stomping the ground in bare-footed liberation. She stands, masked and primal, on a beach, facing the daunting ocean wave in flippant disregard. This card tells us that it's more than okay for women to make noise, stand their ground, make a point, kick butt, and confront their adversaries and the world with courage, self-confidence, and conviction. "You go, Girl!" says Temperance.

15 Devil

That which we worship, which we feel is most important in life, often binds us. This is the message from this card, stark and clear. As women, we are chained to so many of life's cubbyholes, society demanding that we be successful in all of these areas and in all of our endeavors, maintaining standards that are not realistic or attainable for most of us. The Devil warns us about living life as though we are reciting a poem by rote. This card challenges us to break the mold, to cross the line, to take risks, to dare to be who we really are. And who we really are so often goes against the norms of a patriarchal mostly Christian society. The Devil warns us about going with the grain, digging our own ruts and then complaining about them as we stumble along. This card is a mirror of what our lives will be like if we don't undo the chains that bind. It encourages us to seek freedom, freedom of thought and expression, desire and will.

16 Tower

Is she going to jump, or is the female figure perched on the edge of the Tower, surrounded by lightning bolts, going to leap? Not to crash to the ground, but to soar through the stormy sky with a cocky victorious I-knew-I-could-do-it attitude. This card reminds us that when adversity strikes, we are not alone, whatever the decisions we make, there below we will see our sisters gathered together to show their support, offer their encouragement, carry us when need be, and allow us to soar solo when this is to our benefit. The Tower card in the Motherpeace tarot tells us that no matter how bad something looks, we can successfully deal with it.

17 Star

The female figure on this card, submerged peacefully in a natural pool, surrounded by stones, morning glories, a hawk, lotus blossoms and a gentle rain, speaks to us of peace and satisfaction. She speaks to us about learning to become comfortable with ourselves in a variety of settings and situations, whether we are part of a couple, or whether we are alone, whether we have the support of a close family, or whether we face the world independently and on our own terms. The hawk encourages us to continue life's adventure and seek wisdom; the morning glories, beautiful as they are, remind us not to get embroiled and trapped so deeply by life's problems and responsibilities that we lose the essence of our identity; the lotus blossoms highlights the feminine within us and around us, through divinity; and the gentle rain cleanses us and comforts our soul.

18 Moon

Intuition; mystery; the feminine mysteries; the element of Water and all it encompasses: dreams, visions, second sight, the ethereal; the spiral dance; the psyche caught in never-ending cycles of highs and lows, discoveries and enlightenment. The Moon in this deck touches on the basic feminine instincts and the Goddess. It is a meditative journey in and of itself, and in the end, it leaves room for self-discovery and growth.

19 Sun

This card is overwhelmed by the color yellow, and with it the impression of a party, a happy gathering of souls, an endless beach in an endless summer. It speaks of magickal moments frozen in positive energy: The Garden of Eden; your 17th summer; a single moment of successful group co-operation; a magkical joining of hands and ideas to push forward practical positive changes. The traditional meaning for this card is "happiness", and that's exactly what the Sun emphasizes in the Motherpeace deck: happiness for the sake of happiness, one moment from a lifetime that is accepted without question and enjoyed for what it is, perhaps stored away for future reference, when the clouds return to cast their shadows.

20 Judgment

The mystery of the Egyptian ankh overwhelms this card. Its image hovers over that of the earth, radiating the colors of the rainbow, the colors of the chakras, encompassing the world. Unlike traditional decks, Judgment in Motherpeace feels like a soothing balm, bringing a return to balance, a sense of equilibrium that may have been lost and is found again. It's like a balancing of the chakras for the entire world population, and for the physical earth itself. This is a healing card in Motherpeace and the only Judgment card that I've ever liked.

21 World

The image on this card is a woman in a loose-fitting yellow dress and head scarf, clutching a tambourine in one hand and a flaming torch in the other. Around her is a ring, a circle, the symbol of that which is eternal. This ring is made up of one naked figure after the other, each connecting with the next one. This card speaks to us of our lineage, our heritage, the ancestors. It centers on the idea of completion, but not completion with finality, more a sense of the eternal and unending cycle of birth, life, death, and rebirth. And in the center of the circle, the woman is smiling. "This is how it's suppose to be," she is telling us.

Swords

Air/East/Projective Energy

Ace

A diamond in the rough. Beginnings. The figure on this card is sitting in a lotus position within diamond-shaped boxes, light radiating from behind her. All that you touch will turn to gold, but unlike Midas and his curse, your touch will not turn anything to stone. Your touch will ignite a passion and a flurry of communication, discovery, creativity, and power. The magickal sword, Excalibur, is yours for the taking, this card tells us. You simply have to reach out and believe in yourself.

Two

What magickal energy! The female figure on this card is standing in a yoga position (the tree, I believe). She's holding a white feather in each hand, creating the symbol for infinity in the air all about her. Beside her stands a stork, also on one foot. They are on a shore, beneath the full moon, discovering their balance, testing themselves, finding their point of origin, their center. Birth; fertility; unspoken communication; learning about oneself in a moment of solitude; preparing and applying ourselves for the big picture, not just the moment or the immediate future; thinking ahead; gaining perspective. That's what the Two of Swords is all about in Motherpeace. We learn best, this card tells us, when we listen.

Three

The three of swords is a card of scattered and dangerous energy. It warns of conflict, pain, betrayal, and emotional anguish at various levels. Betrayal may be the worst of the disclosures here. Being mentally stung and struck by someone in whom we had complete trust ruptures our ability to recognize just who we may or may not trust. It collapses all trust, like a house of cards with no solid foundation. When the Three of Swords appears, a chain, a connection, is broken, often irreparably. The sense of betrayal will have to be worked through, and everyone will have a different idea about how to do this. The most important thing is not to allow this betrayal to contaminate other relationships, other connections, or the possibility of new connections.

Four

The female figure seated in the center of the pyramid is meditating on nature's balance within her body, a balance that translates to the mind and spirit. She's in touch with the essence of an energy connected to her chakras. You can see behind her, speared on a golden rod, the circular color-co-ordinated spheres for these energy centers. Four is all about balance, but in this case, it is the supreme object in the Four of Swords. It's about balance of body, mind, and spirit; it's about balance between all seven of our main chakras; it's about carrying this balance through into all areas of our lives; it's about stopping to center ourselves, to heal ourselves, to nurture ourselves; it's about making sure that we take care of ourselves in order to take care of others. *"Find your center,"* calmly says the Four of Swords.

Five

The image on this card is a pentacle constructed of swords, and within the center is a wasp. The wasp is as trapped upon this card as the individual for whom this card speaks. We can be trapped by many things, and most of those things involve conflict, which leads to chaos, which leads to confusion, which leads to ineptitude and lassitude. The wasp on this card finds herself sitting inert and impotent in the center of this pentacle, trapped by the swords: harsh words, cutting comments, selfishness, thoughtlessness, the inability to compromise, stubbornness. You will need to find that still center of yourself that speaks in whispers and ethereal images. You will need to find that still center that has the power to reach out and still the chaos that surrounds you, only then will you be free of the trap.

Six

This card reels with the energy and idea of freedom. "Let loose!" the Six of Swords says. Try new things, break new ground, stretch yourself to discover new potential and to develop your talents to the utmost. The essence of the Six of Swords is freedom in wild, unadulterated abandonment. It is the collective energy of our sisters, connecting the universe and harnessing its incredible energy for sheer happiness. Within this card we learn that our individual strength is expansive, explosive, magickal; but when women come together and work for something in unison, the universe will not be able to stop or contain the strength of our will. This card connects you to your sisters, your ancestors, your peers. The Six of Swords implies that we can do great things in large numbers. It implies that everything we do touches everyone we know, including those who are connected to us indirectly. The Six of Swords challenges us to soar.

Seven

The Seven of Swords is a card that inspires us with wisdom, hindsight, determination, strength, and the idea that we, as women, are responsible for protecting ourselves. Not every woman has a knight-in-shining-armor stored in her hall closet, not every woman has someone to stand up for her, not every woman has the love and support of a family. *But every woman has the ability to defend herself successfully.* Grow some balls, this card says, don't just stand around like a deer in the headlights when action is needed for defense. Make sure your boundaries are strengthened, your space is secure, and your guard is up. This isn't about being paranoid and defensive, it's about doing necessary things to protect yourself.

Eight

Progression is still progression, no matter the speed at which you are advancing, no matter the speed at which you are completing your tasks. Once in a while, along life's path, our journey may be temporarily halted by unexpected obstacles. So often we feel that this stop, this temporary cessation of forward movement, is the signal of defeat. On the contrary, once the obstacle as been resolved or annihilated, forward progression will resume at its previous pace, or maybe even at a faster pace, because we've learned something along the way, we've come up with a solution, we solved a problem, we created a positive outcome.

Nine

So many of the swords have to do with confrontation and protection. In a way the Nine of Swords is advising us to be prepared to defend ourselves, a theme that seems to run through this series. But there's more here. This card highlights our path in life, all the twists and turns, the detours, and the dead-ends. This card tells us that life is unpredictable, and that 80% of it will be perfect and happy, or ordinary and safe; but the last 20% is what is going to catch us off guard, and this is what we have to be ready for. This card warns us against getting so wrapped up in the small percentage, the little things, the glitches and bumps, that we miss the big picture. We won't appreciate what we have, we won't meet our full potential because we get side-tracked. Stay on course, as much as you can, the Nine of Swords says. Wander just enough to discover, be distracted just enough to learn.

Ten

In all decks, this card has dire meanings attached to it. In Motherpeace it's even more significant. This card is a warning, a warning to all women everywhere: "What affects one woman impacts **All** women." Remember this. Remember this when your tongue gets ready to turn a black word against one of your sisters; remember this when gossip runs amok, when there's favoritism involved; remember this, that there's two sides to every story; remember that there's safety and strength in numbers; remember that as women we owe loyalty and an allegiance to women all over the world, not just women we have personal contact with. This card is a reminder, a reminder to all women everywhere. We have to stick together. We have to support each other. We have to respect each other. We have to love one another.

Daughter

The image on this card highlights a female figure standing on a rock, bracing herself in the wind, hair flying, sword poised to strike, a group of animals huddled below her, under her protection. It confirms to us woman's dominion over the animal kingdom, the magickal, nurturing, spiritual, mystical connection that so many women just naturally share. It highlights, with the image of a Holy Stone, woman's connection to the world of fairy, and the spiritual connection that so many of us have with the paranormal, with magical creatures and disembodied spirits. It reminds us of the significance and power that comes with intuition and psychic ability. The Daughter of Swords tells us that we are the protectors and keepers of Mother Earth. It reinforces the idea that the ability to nurture is what adds to our mysticism, our heart, our femininity. This card reminds us that we are strong, lest we forget.

Son

The lone male figure on this card, a hunter coming home with newly caught game in his hand, surrounded by a ring of red and white roses, epitomizes the men in our family: our husbands, sons, uncles, and brothers. It reflects on the honor of good men, those men who are endowed with the wonderful instinct to protect, cherish, and love the women in their lives. It celebrates their ambition, their sense of purpose, their stability, and their loyalty. It shines the light on the valor of good men and the principles they stand for.

Priestess

This Priestess of Swords is standing in a pure white world and appears to have released a white owl into the barren landscape. She is sending forth wisdom into the world, and the wisdom that she's sending forth brings back blessings and magick upon her. This card speaks of calmness and simplicity. The Priestess of Swords is sure of her own power and that of the higher energies she invokes. She's comfortable in her solitude, whole within herself. She carries the essence of the Crone within her and all the shadows and intuition that follow the Crone upon her journey through the third stage of life.

Shaman

The Shaman of Swords is all about the voice: learning to find it, to use it, to hone it, and to create an instrument of profound communication with this gift. This card is also a warning, a warning that what can be used to build up can also be used to tear down. The voice can be misused as an instrument of destruction, and if we are to succeed in our endeavors, if we are to build our world and our life in the process, we must learn to use the gift of our voice wisely. This card is tapping us on the shoulder, reminding us that what we say may come back to haunt us, telling us gently to use discretion and kindness, wisdom and restraint.

Wands

Fire/South/Projective Energy

Ace

Aces are beginnings, and they usually appear as a doorway that you can calmly walk through to begin at the beginning of whatever. But this card, in the Motherpeace deck, is different. It's explosive. The image of this card is a blue egg that has cracked wide open in a fiery blaze, and what has hatched from this egg is an individual. This image has its back to us, arms and legs splayed out, thrown with such violence from the egg, she was. This card challenges us to leave all that makes us feel safe and protected behind. It dares us to break new ground, try new things, and to explore the world in brave abandon. This card, the Ace of Wands, says: "Look out world, here I come!"

Two

The Two of Wands speaks of mutual co-operation with our fellow sisters, of working together to achieve a mutually beneficial goal. This card tells us to not only look within ourselves to find the answers, but to look to our older and wiser sisters, to look to those who hold the knowledge and experience that we need. The Two of Wands in this deck reminds us of our ancestors, the wisdom of the ancient ones, the sisters who have passed before us. It speaks of lineage, tradition, and continuity within ourselves and the feminine community.

Three

A woman has many irons in the fire, this card tells us. It represents the busy life of a woman in the midst of raising children, balancing work, spouses, goals, aspirations, and responsibilities to the world at large. This card reminds us that as we drain ourselves of energy for all these tasks, all this responsibility, we must also replenish ourselves. The Three of Wands is a card chock full of energy: ambition, determination, a sense of accomplishment, and pride. Revel in it.

Four

Jubilation, celebration…"*The Gathering*". The image on this card, a band of naked women in garlands, ceremoniously trailing more garlands throughout four poles, is reminiscent of the images from Z Budapest's famous women's gatherings. It bristles of unbridled joy, emancipation, a total abandonment of conventionality and self-consciousness. It speaks of feminine power, happiness, joy, and celebration. The small blue hummingbird, streaking across the top of this card, whispers… "*Freedom!*"

Five

This card is a warning to all womanhood. "Don't bicker among yourselves," it says. "A divided house falls," it reminds us. "Stick together, support and encourage one another," this card admonishes us.

Women tend to be catty with other women. You hear this all the time, and so often it is painfully true. In behaving this way, in not supporting or even undermining our sisters, we are turning our back on all womanhood. We are sabotaging ourselves. Women need other women; and we need them to be supportive, loving, encouraging, and faithful. Stop the catty behavior, the Five of Wands tells us. "Unite, women of the world," this card says.

Six

The main message of this card is to fully accept ourselves as women, to embrace our stark raw female sexuality, which most of the conventional world, ruled by patriarchal religions, does not understand and often even fears. The character on this card invites us to look at ourselves from new perspectives, maybe from intimate views and vantage points that might make us uncomfortable. We've been told so long that we shouldn't go there. We've been told what is acceptable as part of being a woman, and what is not. This card invites us – no, this card **dares** us – to explore our femaleness, to revel in our strengths, to banish any weakness, to grow, to learn, to reach.

Seven

It's all about gathering and organizing. The group of women on this card have obviously come together for a purpose. The center figure seems to be in charge. The Seven of Wands is all about organizing ourselves as a group, being able to pick out women who make strong leaders. It's about getting our ducks in a row to accept life's challenges. It's about being prepared for the unexpected. But not all women have the luxury of being close to a group, and in this there is the sense that even as an individual without a good support system, you can still organize yourself to handle whatever life happens to throw at you. Perhaps this card is trying to emphasize that within us all resides the spirit of our ancestors, the spirit of survival, the spirit of the warrior.

Eight

The Eight of Wands is always about movement, movement and energy. The energy of this card urges us to shoot off as much as we can: work, projects, ideas, activities. The Eight of Wands speaks of movement and unbridled energy that needs to be focused. It speaks of too much for one person to do, of goals that might seem unattainable yet help us to reach new plateaus of creativity and success. Sometimes, when so many people are telling us we can't accomplish something, we have to believe in ourselves and forge ahead with bluster and bravado, having faith in ourselves when no one else seems to.

Nine

In quiet contemplation, you will find your strength. The female figure on this card, sitting naked and cross-legged ahead of a row of flaming wands, a coiled snake on each side of her, is calm in the face of adversity, versatile in the midst of life's unexpected situations. This card emphasizes the importance of our inner calm, our inner voice, the balancing of our energies (the chakras). This card, though awash in a red background, alight with the flames of nine torches, represents wisdom and grace, and quiet dignity.

Ten

This card portrays a group of naked women caught up in a frenzy of music and dance. It highlights community and working together, it highlights sisterhood and group worship of feminine divinity. The Ten of Wands in ordinary decks represents burdens, but in the Motherpeace deck we realize that as long as we have sisters, mothers, aunts, and friends, there is nothing that we can't tackle and be victorious over. It is within the worldwide community of womanhood that strength and power, joy and hope, accomplishment and poise are raised to new levels and realized.

Daughter

This card carries the energy of wild abandonment in the midst of carefree youth. The energy of the Daughter of Wands is a reminder to us not to lose this wild, sometimes frenetic, extremely powerful energy with age. We don't have to lose it, really! Exuberance, expectation, enthusiasm are timeless; it is this very energy which gets things done, gets accomplishments met. This is a powerful card filled with movement, from the geese in the air, streaking along with intention and purpose, to the unicorned goat racing beneath them, and the female figure, arms flung above her head, bounding through time and space.

Son

The energy of the Daughter is carried over to the energy of the Son, but it's different, it's not as solitary and singular, it encompasses community and family. It is the springboard inspiring cooperation. "Dance this dance with me," says the Son of Wands. The figure on this card is dancing for the female figures of the family, enticing them to join him, acting as motivational inspiration. In the midst of life, this card reminds us, we don't have to do everything alone. There's strength and power in numbers, where goals are set and met. "But life can still be fun," says the Son of Wands, with a wry smile.

Priestess

From the rainbow above her, to the large silent cat beside her, this card speaks of the Priestess as "Caretaker", a guardian of the earth and its creatures. In the Priestess of Wands is quiet dignity, compassion, the iconic symbol of the "Mother's Touch". But she is not burdened by these roles, in fact, this Priestess finds quiet strength in caring for others, in giving of herself. She is the epitome of "Mother", sacrifice is her way. It's the energy of this card that will bring you peace, comfort, happiness, solace in times of grief, serenity in times of unrest.

Shaman

The Shaman of Wands is all about control, keeping it, losing it, suffering the consequences of it. This Shaman has all those things he loves gathered around himself, kept close and tight, thinking that he's protecting his precious belongings and people. However, just the opposite is true. The Shaman of Wands tries so carefully to keep those things which are important to him close and controlled, that he often winds up smothering the very things he's trying to protect. This Shaman is resilient. The phoenix rising from the ashes behind the figure on this card is very fitting. The Shaman of Wands will bounce back, recover and recoup, from the most devastating experiences.

Cups

Water/West/Receptive Energy

Ace

The character on this card is taking a swan dive into a huge fountain of water. Sitting complacently before this fountain are two swans. Aces are all about beginnings, and this Ace is all about relationships. This card reminds us that you never know what you're going to find, what it's going to be like, when you enter into a new relationship with someone, whether this be a romantic relationship or a friendship. We trust on faith, and this card tells us that's okay. Don't hang back from beginning a new friendship or relationship just because you've been hurt in the past. Don't let your bad experiences rob you of something beautiful in your future. That's what this card is telling us.

Two

Partnership, pairing, and sharing. As much as our individuality is respected and held sacred, so is our ability to share our lives, our world, our bodies, and ourselves with another human being. Whether we are mated to someone through romantic love, creative endeavors, ideas, familial connections, or simply choice, this is a sacred union because what is part of us is touching another individual, adding to the experience of their life in ways we might not even realize. The fluidity of relationships is highlighted with this card, represented by the ocean and a pair of dolphins interacting on a blue horizon. Partnerships are not stagnant and are constantly metamorphosing to encompass change, changes within the partnership itself and changes to the individuals. Because of its fluidity, partnerships, friendships, and special connections may not always be forever, but may touch our lives at a moment when it is most needed, when this connection will be most beneficial.

Three

"Let's celebrate!" says the Three of Cups. As women, let's celebrate our wisdom, our knowledge, our humanity, our beauty, our similarities, our differences, our strengths, and our weaknesses. Let's celebrate with music and dance, with food and company. Let's celebrate our diversity, embracing all womanhood, all cultures, all religions. Don't let our differences divide us, this card reminds us. Womanhood united is so much stronger than womanhood divided.

Four

The character on this card is standing, vulnerable and naked, caught on the beach between the tides, surrounded by four cups. Traditionally this is the card that forces us to face unpleasant issues and personal demons, and that's shown here where our vulnerability and delicate nature are highlighted in a breath-taking and shattering way. Which way do we turn? Which direction do we take? What if we make the wrong choice? How often are we frozen by inaction, caught in the ebb and flow of life, unable to move forward or backward? The hesitancy and dilemma of the human condition is the focal point of this card. We're left to question all that we are, all that we've been, all that we trust, in order to move on with our lives.

Five

We all retreat within our own shell. Whether single or married, mother or not, in solitude we discover our inner being, our strengths and our weaknesses, our promise, and our vulnera-bility. And as we metamorphose throughout this lifetime, sliding from one stage to another, often barely noticing the transition (and at other times jolted by the shock of it), we must constantly change shells, always seeking a larger one. This card is a card of personal growth and discovery, transmutations that lead us to the soul's final incarnation.

Six

Three women on steeds are riding the crest of an ocean wave to shore, holding aloft flaming torches. The Six of Cups is all about the highs and lows of life, about overcoming obstacles and sticking with a challenge till you come out on top. It's all about learning from our mistakes. It's about taking the negative experiences of our lives and using them to our advantage. It's about holding our own in this world, till we gain victory over everything that bogs us down.

Seven

This card is traditionally a card of decisions, and Motherpeace affirms that decisions we make must be made from our own feminine intuition and convictions. This card also speaks to us of responsibility, for decisions that a woman makes affects so many in the worldwide circle around her: friends, acquaintances, family, husband, children are all impacted. The Seven of Cups also reminds us that, although we should trust our own intuition when making decisions, there is also a higher power from which we can draw strength and wisdom. The image on this card includes a woman in the center with a cup and a dove on her head, indicating that all decisions made will send forth energy and reverberations through her life and the world, and it will also bring this energy back to where it originated, coming full circle. Think carefully, decide wisely.

Eight

The eight of cups in Motherpeace is an octopus, tentacles outstretched, and each one filled with a piece of pottery, a coffee cup, a pitcher, an empty vessel of some kind. How well this pertains to a woman's life! We are multi-taskers, juggling husbands, work, children, and myriad other possibilities in the palm of our hand (and inside our full and busy brain). "You are super-human!" society tells us, our culture tells us, and sometimes we tell ourselves. But wait. This octopus, floating in the calm blue waters of the ocean, needs to be able to let go of everything it's holding, to let go of everything it's holding back. This card is telling us that we need time, still, quiet time to ourselves, in order to regain perspective, in order to find our center.

Nine

Enjoy! Reap the rewards you deserve. This is a beautiful delight-fully hedonistic card. It depicts several naked women around a pool, obviously in the throes of enjoying life at its leisure. Each woman is immersed in the unabashed joy of living, the joy of personal rest, the joy of desired activity, the joy of daydreaming, the joy of solitude, the joy of company. You deserve those things you wish for, those things you've worked for, those moments of human bliss. Graciously accept this gift from the universe, with no strings attached.

Ten

In traditional decks the Ten of Cups is all about family, in Motherpeace, it's bigger. It's all about community. It's about women banding together, working together, supporting each other, contributing to the world we live in, contributing to the future of our society, contributing to the spiritual energy of the Goddess. The cup runneth over, the path is laid open and clear for the multitudes. Female energy is celebrated. We are magnified. "We" as in us, the women of the world. Celebrate and rejoice. Embrace the power.

Daughter

The character upon this card is washing herself in a pool of water beneath a waterfall, arms and legs extended, delighting in the purifying coolness. The Maiden and beginnings seem to be highlighted, the excitement of fresh starts, the satisfaction of clean slates. This Maiden is washed clear of regrets, able to look forward and to start at the beginning of a new journey. Her hand rests upon a large placid turtle, and perhaps it's this creature that will remind her to take her time, move slowly, think long and hard before making decisions, so as not to repeat past-life mistakes. On the bank of the shore, a lone tree is growing, bending in towards the pool and the Maiden. This is the Tree of Knowledge, or perhaps the spirit of a guide, who will offer wisdom to the Maiden as she begins this new journey.

Son

The Son of Cups speaks of new relationships, and not necessarily conventional relationships. It also speaks of growth, fertility, self-analysis, and enlightenment. It brings you at once to a place of inner peace, and it's this inner peace that will affect the fabric of the numerous relationships we have in our lives. This card also asks us to take a stark look at the male figures around us, how we relate to them, and what type of energy is generated through this association. The essence of this card is "Discovery": discovery of ourselves, the intimacies and intricate patterns of the personalities around us, and how we weave this all into our persona and our daily lives.

Priestess

This Priestess encourages us to embrace our natural gifts, our natural abilities. This card celebrates the element of Water and all that this means. "Be still," it says, "Listen... shhhh. What do you hear?" The small sounds of the world; the sound of rain in the trees; the sound of a cat purring; the sound of a sleeping infant's breath; the sound of that still voice in your head, the voice you may have heard all your life, but avoided, the voice you may have heard all your life without a full realization of exactly what it was. It is you. "Be still and listen," says the Priestess of Cups.

Shaman

Pisces; seeking; inward journeys; dreams; and intuition... This Shaman represents our eternal quest to understand the unknown, to see the invisible, to experience the world of spiritual miracles and impossibilities. This Shaman takes us on an inward journey to find ourselves and to become familiar with the entities that inhabit this plane of existence... old ghosts and new personas.

Discs

Earth/North/Receptive Energy

Ace

This card is all about discovery, and it's about discovery of the most personal intimate aspects of ourselves, through mind, body, and spirit. It reaches to the depth of our most secret selves, and it involves the process of learning to share this aspect of our persona with those we love. The Ace of Disks demands that we strip down, literally and figuratively, and learn about ourselves at very basic levels. This card encompasses self-love and approval, fertility, and an integration of the masculine into our lives in uplifting and positive ways, embracing the energy and strength we find there. This card is about bonding with and accepting our wild side, that irrepressible nature that means survival and success.

Two

Woman is the epitome of balance. In modern times she most often inhabits both worlds: that of the outside, involving work and community; and that of the inside, the world of hearth and home. We look to Woman for stability and reassurance. As the wheels turn and life progresses from one stage and phase to another, so she moves with it, balancing creativity (and sometimes children) on one hip, while she holds responsibility on the other. It is from this balance she creates that those around her are able to live and work, love and play, on an even keel, with feet planted firmly on solid ground.

Three

"Climb the ladder to success," this card tells us. "Be all that you can be." The Three of Discs is traditionally all about work, your employment, your job, your career. But this deck, as usual, takes it so much further. The Motherpeace Three of Discs is giving womanhood a thumbs-up. It's telling us that we can accomplish whatever we put our minds to. It's telling us to dream big, set high goals, set high standards. We can do it! We can accomplish it; we can meet it; we are smart and strong enough to take our place at the front of life's class.

Four

Sometimes we have to set boundaries, and this is not only okay, but necessary. Sometimes we have to protect those things we find precious, those things that belong to us; whether this be material items, relationships, ideas, or personal freedoms. The four of discs tells us that it's okay to say "No". It's okay to keep what belongs to us, even if the rest of society is telling us we must share, telling us we must give and give and give. This card warns us not to give so much that we deplete our own resources. This card tells woman to protect that which belongs to her, that which she has worked to create, that which she holds precious, that which gives her strength.

Five

Fortitude and ingenuity... it's these traits that will get you through a difficult time, and it's these traits that will strengthen your resolve to be successful. Having the self-confidence and self-esteem to know that you can accomplish what you start out to do, to know that you are capable of taking care of yourself, even under adverse conditions, to know that you will come through a trial stronger than you were when you began the journey is a lesson in personal empowerment. This card teaches us independence, as it enables us to depend upon ourselves.

Six

Woman's ability and responsibility to care for others is highlighted in this card, but so is her exquisite gift to accomplish this. The image is that of a caretaker, bending to place her healing hands on the body of someone in need, someone in need of magick, someone in need of Woman's Gift. As the six discs surrounding this image vibrate with energy, appearing to spin and weave with the universal web, we can feel the Gift. We can feel the healing energy, we can feel woman's destiny and all that she contributes to the world and the individuals around her. Caretaker, Mother, Goddess, Healer, Witch, Wise-Woman... they are all us.

Seven

The pregnant female figure, languidly resting amongst a vine of plump ripe watermelons, says it all. *Reap the harvest, enjoy your bounty.* You are rich and fertile. You are ripe and luscious: physically fertile, as in the material world and all that you have gained; emotionally and mentally fertile, as in alive with ideas, plans, and creative projects. The universe is yours, the Seven of Discs says. This card also tells us to relax and enjoy. Stop and take the time to appreciate and fully experience your success.

Eight

Laboring, whether the solitary woman laboring to give birth, or a community of women laboring for a single cause, they will accomplish a miracle. Within this deck, the Eight of Discs is a card highlighting effort, co-operation, single-mindedness, determination, and divine inspiration. It emphasizes woman's life work, it spotlights her creativity, talent, and ingenuity. It emphasizes both our personal apprenticeship to life, as well as our community responsibility.

Nine

Contentment, wisdom, experience, a coming-of-age is the theme for the Nine of Discs. The beautiful figure in the center of this card, crowned with abundant gray hair drawn gracefully back, is surrounded by magickal objects and tools. She's practicing her craft, working her magick, conjuring the spirits, moving energy through the universe. She is calm, self-assured, self-reliant, self-contained. She is who she is... *"I Am Who I Am"*. At this point in life, she is not seeking answers, but instead finds other women coming to her for advice, knowledge, and instruction. The Crone has arrived, says the Nine of Discs.

Ten

On this card you see a circle of women, a wide variety of women, from many cultures and ethnicities. In the center of this circle is a naked woman giving birth, the child just emerging from her body. On both sides, she is supported by a woman, held up in their arms. The traditional meaning for the Ten of Pentacles in a standard deck is wealth, usually familial wealth. The idea of wealth still holds with the Ten of Discs in the Motherpeace deck, but it's a different kind of wealth. This card tells us to embrace the wealth of our sisters in the form of their knowledge, compassion, wisdom, and connection to the sacred feminine. This card magnifies the unity of the women of the world and the power and strength generated by this familial connection.

Daughter

The female warrior, the strength of youth and feminine vitality, are highlighted by the Daughter of Discs. In the Motherpeace deck, this is a card of affirmation. It's telling us to remember that we are a fountain of strength and possibilities. The image of this card is that of a young and naked warrior priestess within a sacred circle. She's holding aloft a staff that is emanating power and magickal energy. She is the one directing this energy; she is the one in charge of herself and the situation. Remember this, the Daughter of Discs tells us: *"You are in control!"*

Son

The warrior is also highlighted as the Son of Discs, but in a different way than the Daughter; there is a different nuance here. The energy of this card suggests self-sufficiency, the idea of providing for your material needs, the idea of perfection in all that we do which comes through practice, determination, and our own unique talents. This card is telling us to fine-tune our craft, whatever that may be for each of us, hone your skills. The Son of Discs tells us: *"When you think you've done something to the best of your ability, you'll find out that you can do even more."*

Priestess

This Priestess is rooted to the earth and the Earth, both the physical body and the element. She represents reproduction, creativity, and fertility of womanhood in all aspects of her life and her being. She is life come full circle, completion, accomplishment, and willpower. This Priestess is calm in the face of adversity. This Priestess is the foundation of the family. She speaks to us in the language of the old fertility goddesses, embellishing the story of creation from the feminine aspect. All who are lost, discouraged, weary, or sad can find encouragement and new energy with the Priestess of Discs.

Shaman

The Shaman on this card is seated on his steed, slowly making his way between desert rock formations. At his back is a sunrise or a sunset. To his right is an eagle, and in his left hand he holds a shield. This card carries about it an overwhelming sense of peace and calm. The Shaman is making this solitary journey with no fear or trepidation, open to all that he will experience and willing to learn from it. As he journeys through the beautiful, but barren landscape, we are reminded that this is how we should journey through life. Whether the sun at his back is rising or setting, he'll meet it at the next horizon.

Part 8

Wise-Woman Wisdom

The following section contains correspondences for working rituals and magick. Let's get one thing clear for anyone who is new to Goddess spirituality and "New-Age" ideas. Labels can be misleading, intimidating, or even frightening to the average individual. Some people might refer to the practices printed in this book as witchcraft, or hoodoo, or Wicca, green witchcraft, or some other awesome sounding mysterious name; and all of these names might correctly apply on various levels, and then again, none of them might apply. There's no label required for any of this, really.

I consider this "Energy Work", a spiritual path that centers on the Goddess.

And that's all it is.

That's all magick is basically – energy work, *the manipulation of energy to manifest desired results in our lives.* It's that plain and simple. If you decide to practice this sort of spirituality, I can guarantee you that no dark bogeyman will come popping out of the woodwork to snatch your soul away. All that will come of it is a deeper understanding of yourself, a more solid connection to the divine, and an inner sense of peace.

Colors

Red
Chakra: Root chakra
Element: Fire
Day: Tuesday (Mars)
Magick: Spells for love, lust, passion, pure energy, clearing and cleansing, speeding matters along, male issues, God energy

Orange
Chakra: Sacral chakra
Day: Sunday (the sun)
Magick: God energy, healing, success fertility magick, spells for Mars energy, sun energy, male issues (a milder energy than red)

Yellow
Chakra: Solar plexus
Element: Air
Day: Wednesday (Mercury)
Magick: Spells for communication, opening new avenues, success with mental endeavors, fairy magick, beginnings, creativity, the muses

Green
Chakra: Heart chakra
Element: Earth
Day: Friday (Venus)
Magick: Spells for money, wealth, health and healing, material matters, physical issues, growth, fertility, female issues, Goddess energy

Blue

Chakra: Throat chakra

Element: Water

Day: Monday (Moon)

Magick: Spells for the realms of dreams, psychism – clairvoyance, clairsentience, clairaudience; to induce visions, to enhance divination, Goddess energy, moon energy, mysticism, female issues, wishes

Purple

Chakra: Crown chakra

Day: Thursday (Jupiter)

Magick: Legal issues, financial issues, money and business, expansion, to enhance understanding between two individuals or groups, contracts, psychic magick, spirituality

Black

Day: Saturday (Saturn)

Magick: Spells for banishing, gray magick, cleansing, exorcism

White

Use white for purification. White can also be a substitute for any other color.

Numbers

1. One

Planet: Sun
Element: Fire
Letters: A, J, S
Major Arcana[4]: The Magician
Energies: Developing the self, the All, wholeness, unity, beginnings

2. Two

Planet: Moon
Element: Water
Letters: B, K, T
Major Arcana: High Priestess
Energies: Duality, balance, couples, partnerships

3. Three

Planet: Jupiter
Element: Fire
Letters: C, L, U
Major Arcana: Empress
Energies: Health, triple aspects, psychism

4. Four

Planet: Uranus
Element: Air
Letters: D, M, V
Major Arcana: Emperor
Energies: Quarters, foundations, the elements

5. Five

Planet: Mercury
Element: Air

Letters: E, N, W
Major Arcana: Hierophant
Energies: Communication, fulfillment

6. Six
Planet: Venus
Element: Water
Letters: F, O, X
Major Arcana: The Lovers
Energies: Emotions, magnetism, gods/goddesses, cats

7. Seven
Planet: Neptune
Element: Water
Letters: G, P, Y
Major Arcana: Chariot
Energies: Intuition, psychism, the dark side, shadow

8. Eight
Planet: Saturn
Element: Earth
Letters: H, Q, Z
Major Arcana: Justice
Energies: Material aspects, travel, protection, discipline

9. Nine
Planet: Mars
Element: Fire
Letters: I, R
Major Arcana: Crone
Energies: Aggression, conflict, dominance

Planets[5]

Sun

The magickal energy of the Sun centers around the illumination and brilliance of the God. This is exactly the energy you need for healing: healing of the body, the mind, healing of relationships, healing from trauma. It's the energy of rehabilitation. It also contains that spark of potent masculine in-your-face, I-am-wonderful, kick-up-your-heels and rejoice magick for personal inspiration and self-empowerment. Use the magick of the Sun for the men in your life, to empower them, to heal them, to purify them, to clarify them. It is their energy, watch in delight as they run with it.

Moon

The Moon embodies the Goddess. It is all enveloping for any female issues. It rises to a sacred wise-woman level that will take you to new heights of spiritual awareness and personal growth. It is the most empowering energy used for women. The Moon embraces the element of Water and moves with the tides of the Earth. This is the energy of the priestess, the spiritual feminist, the witch. The magick of the Moon is connected to womanhood throughout her entire life, helping her to transition along the way, from maiden to mother to crone. The Moon will move with you, a soft hand on your shoulder, a gentle guide throughout your life. Embrace her.

Mercury

As the god Mercury speeds through the air, clearing the way for concise communication and creativity, so the energy of this planet will work for you in the same way. The mind, the most elusive, ethereal, mysterious part of us is embodied within the element of this planet and the magick that it creates. This is the planet and the magick for all artists, writers, those who use the eloquence of speech for their work, those who have a message for the world, those individuals whose voice needs to be heard. Speak through the energy of Mercury, send your message with the magick of this planet in complete assurance that you will be heard.

Venus

The name of this planet is synonymous with love and beauty. The energy of this planet is all about relationships, love, friendship, commitment, and the idea of finding unique beauty within each individual – not the shallow surface beauty we're fed within our culture and the media, but the internal beauty that transcends time and transcends age. Use the magick of this planet to enhance or to discover beauty and love that never die, never dim with age, never wither; but beauty and love that continue indefinitely, leaving their imprint on the universe in a million different magickal ways.

Earth

Mother Nature, birth, the physical manifestation of magickal desires... the energy of this planet encompasses those things in the physical world that we covet and relish with hedonistic desire and abandon. But the energy of Earth is deeper than that. It connects us to nature in an incredibly intimate way. We become one with all the other creatures we co-inhabit this planet with. Use this energy to embrace and celebrate our precious planet and all the holy things that live here with us: the flora (the healing herbs and beautiful flowers and sacred trees) and fauna (those animals we share a magickal connection with, our totems, as well as those animals who have graciously allowed us to embrace them as pets).

Mars

The fiery energy of this planet is connected to the spirit of the warrior. It has in-your-face energy that you can invoke for protection, revenge, for justice and retribution. It's the no nonsense unquestionable energy you need for healing, believe it or not. The energy of Mars is the energy you will invoke when you must stand and fight. Remember, when you call upon the energy of these planets, you are not "asking" for assistance or healing, it is a matter of "knowing" that you have the power and the knowledge to manipulate this energy to your own advantage.

Jupiter

Jupiter is all about expansion and growth, usually connected to finances and money, court cases, or anything for that matter that's connected to the judicial system. These are the primary energies for Jupiter. Abundance can be the theme and energy that's invoked here, and the term "abundance" can be used in a very broad spectrum. If there's not enough of something in your life, this is the planet and the energy that you need to rectify the situation.

Saturn

This is the planet with the most notorious reputation, a planet geared for darker energies, a planet revered by those spiritual practitioners who are not afraid to stand their magickal ground, not afraid to retaliate, not afraid to seek protection, not afraid to traverse the gray areas. Saturn is *The Exorcist*. This is the planet whose energy can be invoked to capture or punish "the bad guy", as in sexual predators, criminals who have carried out crimes against the body or mind of innocent individuals. Be sure that the energy you direct from Saturn is justified; the Goddess, in all her wisdom and omnipotence, will know where punishment should rightly fall.

Moon Phases

Watch the phases of the moon and time your magick accordingly.

Waxing Crescent to the Full Moon
Receptive magick. Cast magick to bring something to you.

New Moon to the Waning Crescent
Projective magick. Cast magick to send something from you, to banish.

Days of the Week

Sunday
Planet: Sun
Element: Fire
Number: 1
Crystal/Stone: Amber, yellow topaz
Herb: Marigold, sunflower
Animal: Lion, hawk
Astrological Sign: Leo
Tree: Ash, birch, laurel
Deities: The Goddess, elves
Magick: Health, the God, male issues, spirituality

Monday
Planet: Moon
Element: Water
Number: 2
Crystal/Stone: Moonstone, clear quartz
Herb: Mugwort, willow
Animal: Turtle, dolphin
Astrological Sign: Cancer
Tree: Elder, willow
Deities: Hecate, Crone goddesses
Magick: The Goddess, female issues, dreams, psychism

Tuesday
Planet: Mars
Element: Fire
Number: 9
Crystal/Stone: Ruby, blood stone
Herb: Nettles, bittersweet
Animal: Tiger, falcon

Astrological Sign: Aries, Scorpio
Tree: Holly, elm, cedar
Deities: Hunter gods, elves
Magick: Aggressive energy, marriage, healing disagreements

Wednesday
Planet: Mercury
Element: Air
Number: 5
Crystal/Stone: Citrine, agate
Herb: Slippery elm, moss rose
Animal: Monkey, magpie
Astrological Sign: Gemini, Virgo
Tree: Hazel, forsythia
Deities: The God, the Goddess
Magick: Communication, your muse, spirit connection

Thursday
Planet: Jupiter
Element: Earth
Number: 3
Crystal/Stone: Amethyst, tiger eye
Herb: Mint, patchouli
Animal: horse, eagle
Astrological Sign: Sagittarius, Pisces
Tree: Oak, pine
Deities: The God
Magick: Legal and financial issues, expansion and growth

Friday
Planet: Venus
Element: Water
Number: 6
Crystal/Stone: Rose quartz, jade

Herb: Rose, carnation
Animal: Cat, dove
Astrological Sign: Taurus, Libra
Tree: Birch, apple, myrtle
Deities: The Goddess
Magick: Love, beauty, friendship, goddess energy

Saturday

Planet: Saturn
Element: Earth, Fire
Number: 8
Crystal/Stone: Jet, black onyx
Herb: Wormwood, morning glory
Animal: Raven, black cat
Astrological Sign: Capricorn, Aquarius
Tree: Alder, hawthorn
Deities: Fairies, witches
Magick: Hexing/cursing, protection magick

The Elements

Earth
Dates: December 21 to March 20 (Winter Solstice to eve of Spring Equinox)
Direction: North
Time of Day: 12pm-12am
Energy: Feminine/receptive

Correspondences for Earth
Color: Green
Elemental: Gnomes
Season: Winter
Ritual Tools: Pentacles and salt
Tarot: Pentacles
Zodiac: Taurus, Virgo, Capricorn
Angel: Uriel
Hermetic Axiom: "To know"
Zodiac: Taurus, Virgo, Capricorn

Air
Dates: March 21 to June 20 (Spring Equinox to the eve of Summer Solstice)
Direction: East
Time of Day: Sunrise, 6am
Energy: Masculine/projective

Correspondences for Air
Color: Yellow
Elementals: Sylphs and fairies
Season: Spring
Ritual Tools: Athame, sword
Tarot: Swords

Angel: Raphael
Hermetic Axiom: "To will"
Zodiac: Libra, Aquarius, Gemini

Fire
Dates: June 21 to September 22 (Summer Solstice to the eve of Autumn Equinox)
Direction: South
Time of Day: Noon, 12pm
Energy: Masculine/projective

Correspondences for Fire
Color: Red
Elemental: Salamanders
Season: Summer
Ritual tools: Candle, wand, staff
Tarot: Wands
Angel: Michael
Hermetic Axiom: "To dare"
Zodiac: Aries, Leo, Sagittarius

Water
Dates: September 23 to December 20 (Autumn Equinox to the eve of Winter Solstice)
Direction: West
Time of Day: Sunset, 6pm
Energy: Feminine/receptive

Correspondences for Water
Color: Blue
Elementals: Undines
Season: Autumn
Ritual Tools: Chalice and cauldron
Tarot: Cups

Angel: Gabriel
Hermetic Axiom: "To keep silent"
Zodiac: Cancer, Scorpio, Pisces

Magickal Oils

I'm going to include in this section my own personal recipes for the following magickal oils right out of my very own Book of Shadows, or *"De Big Black Book"* as I like to call it. The ingredients are mostly mundane plants, herbs, spices and such that you probably already have on hand in your kitchen cupboards; but don't be thrown by a more exotic ingredient. You can usually pick up an unusual herb or item at any local new-age or pagan shop. And if you aren't lucky enough to live near a magickal shop, you can try finding such items online.[6]

The Base for Oils

There are a lot of people who insist on using the most expensive oils they can find, but the truth is that this doesn't matter, not really; and if pinching pennies is a must, then go with a cheap bottle of vegetable oil from the grocery store. If you choose, you may use olive oil, or mineral oil, or almond oil, or grape seed oil, or even some other oil that you feel a special affinity towards. In my world, pinching pennies is a necessity, so I opt for the cheap stuff, and it works with absolute gusto, I can assure you.

The Herbs

I'd like to say that when I create my magickal oils, I include the very special power of "3". I use at least *three* types of herbs in each of my oils. You don't need any more than that, really. Of course, if you want to include herbs not only for your magickal intention, but also an herb for the planets, I would add three more herbs to the oil for a total of six. If you choose to include corresponding herbs to the element you're working with, then add three more for a total of nine... the ultimate magickal number. ("By the awful awesome power of 3 x 3," so the incantation goes). But remember, this oil is *your* creation, go with the flow, follow your instincts, don't be afraid to create your own unique magickal oil... Let the Spirit move you.

Some people follow the practice of heating their oils and ingredients just until they catch the scent in order to raise the vibrational energy of the magickal potion, right before adding it to a glass bottle, sort of like giving it a "jump start". Other people simply add the oil and ingredients to a bottle and cap it off. I've done both. To tell you the truth, I've noticed no magickal difference; however, if you believe that this extra step will also imbue your magickal oil with extra strength or direction, then by all means go for it. Experiment with the process and see if you notice any difference for yourself. One last thought... some practitioners will sit their oils out to bathe in the moonlight, or the sunlight, depending upon the energies they're trying to catch. Keep this in mind.

Can you simply go out and buy these magickal oils already made? Yes, you can actually, but I suggest that you learn to make them for yourself. There is no doubt that the personal energy you put into crafting such items adds to their potency, their power, and their effectiveness. All the experience and expertise in the world can't give a love potion as much "oomph" as the creator's own steaming hot lust. Remember, witchcraft is all about energy and the successful manipulation of energy to achieve your desires. The more personal energy you add to your own spells, the more powerful you will be, and the more successful are your magickal endeavors.

Health and Healing Oil

This ointment is used to "dress"[7] candles used in magick for healing, or to maintain continued good health. Good health is everything. If you're ill, or a loved one is sick, nothing else in life is going to matter – nothing. Being healthy is so paramount, so basic, that's the reason I've listed this oil first. If you, or someone close to you, has health issues, use the guidelines below to create the candle magick necessary for healing.

Anoint a *green* candle with this oil for healing of the body; a *yellow* candle for healing of the mind; and a *red* candle for the physical healing of the reproductive system. A yellow and red candle burned together are excellent healing conduits for the mental and emotional healing of sexual abuse victims.

Correspondences and Ingredients

Day: **Monday** (Moon): The reproductive system, female issues; **Wednesday** (Mercury): Mental health issues; **Sunday** (Sun): Physical health issues

Candle Colors: Along with the appropriate candle color for the specific type of healing, as listed in the information above, you can add extra energy to your candle spell by incorporating candles for the planets: **Moon:** Blue or silver; **Mercury:** Yellow; **Sunday:** Yellow or gold

Moon Phase: Waxing to bring good health and healing to you; waning to banish illness

The Base: Vegetable oil, almond oil, or olive oil

The Herbs: **To heal:** Allspice, apple, bay, cinnamon, fennel, gardenia, garlic, ginseng, ivy, mint, mugwort, onion, pine, rose, rosemary, sandalwood, thyme tobacco; **to maintain health:** Coriander, geranium, marjoram, nutmeg, St. John's wort, thyme

My Recipe
Base: Olive oil
Herbs: 3 pinches of rosemary,
3 pinches of sage
3 pinches of St. John's wort

Exorcism/Purification Oil

Don't think of this oil in terms of a Catholic priest and a traditional exorcism. Think of this oil as the witch taking charge of, reclaiming, and cleansing her personal space. Anoint a black candle with this oil to exorcise those demons that are bothering you, whether the irritation is physical or mental, a full-fledged paranormal haunting, or a standard house cleansing to clear sluggish muddy energy. Anoint a white candle with this oil and burn it to purify your physical space or your mental/physical state. I've used this oil to exorcise entities haunting my home, and I've used this oil to exorcise people from my life.

Correspondences and Ingredients

Day: Saturday (Saturn)

Candle Colors: Black (to banish, purge, and exorcise); white (to purify and cleanse)

Moon Phase: Waning

The Base: Vegetable oil, olive oil, mineral oil, cod liver oil

The Herbs: **Exorcism**: Basil, cloves, cumin, cayenne pepper, dragon's blood, garlic, horseradish, lilac, mint, onion, pepper, pine rosemary, sandalwood, yarrow, wormwood; **Purification**: Anise, bay chamomile, fennel, horseradish, lemon grass, lavender, iris, parsley, rosemary, sage, thyme, tobacco, turmeric, valerian

My Recipe

Base: Mineral oil

Herbs: Equal amounts of cloves, sea salt, wormwood

Mars Astrological Oil

The energy of this oil encompasses the power of Mars, the fierceness of the warrior, the wild untamed energy of the element of Fire, and some plain ol' no nonsense kick-ass, in-your-face, stand-your-ground power. This is the oil you need when you are touched with any circumstance that puts you in a "flight or fight" adrenalin rush, and that little voice in your head screams *"Fight!"* This ointment promotes courage, strength, aggression, sexual energy, healing after surgery, exorcisms, and defensive magick. I've found this to be an especially effective and strong magickal tool, and I want to caution you that this oil can also banish. Use it wisely.

Correspondences and Ingredients

Day: Tuesday (Mars) – this oil proves to be most potent when made on a Tuesday, within the astrological hour of Mars, and with the correct coinciding moon phase

Candle Colors: Red, orange

Moon Phase: Waning, to banish; waxing, to bring something to you

The Base: Olive oil

The Herbs: Allspice, basil, cloves, coriander, cumin, garlic, ginger, horseradish, mustard, onion, pepper, radish, tobacco

My Recipe

Base: Olive oil

Herbs: 3 pinches of allspice (or 9 whole allspice)

3 pinches of cumin

3 pinches of cloves (or 9 whole cloves)

1 pinch of ginger if there is a sense of urgency and fast results are needed

Witches' Oil

This is an all-purpose oil that can be used to anoint the body prior to rituals or spell casting. It can also be used to dress candles, or to anoint objects. Witches' Oil can be used to "touch" anything or anyone with a bit of old-world magick. You can create this oil with an energy that tends to be all encompassing, an energy that might be called "generic" when it comes to corre-spondences and intentions. This is a perfect oil to have if you're cramped on space for magickal supplies and can't keep oodles and oodles of bottles and ointments on hand, or if you're pinching pennies.

First, let's keep it simple; let's keep it generic.

Correspondences and Ingredients

Day: Any day convenient for you

Candle Color: Neutral – black or white

Moon Phase: Dark moon

The Base: Whatever oil you have on hand, or an oil you can afford

The Herbs: The basics – rosemary, sage, thyme

My Recipe

3 pinches of rosemary

3 pinches of thyme

3 whole sage leaves

Psychic Oil

Most people think that psychic abilities come naturally and just kick in with no warning, much like they see in the movies and on TV. And this might be true for a few super-gifted individuals in the world, but for the rest of us, who may have spent a lifetime ignoring that little voice in our head, we have to give ourselves a little extra magickal oomph to pick up this information. The average individual does not get two to three-minute flashes (in Full Technicolor, no less) of intuitive information. In actuality, it can be extremely subtle and extremely easy to overlook with all the brain chatter that we have going on. Psychic Oil is simply meant to help us focus much-needed energy on this aspect of ourselves, on our efforts to see what most people never will, on our ability to hear that barely perceptible murmur. Once you've used and strengthened your psychic muscle, you'll find that you'll need this tool less and less.

Anoint your third eye chakra with this oil before doing divination of any kind. Anoint your pendulum, rune stones, divining rod, or any other divination tool that you're using. If it happens to be tarot cards, or some other card deck, don't damage your cards with the oil, but add a touch of the oil to the bag or box where you keep your cards. Anoint and burn a lavender candle dressed with psychic oil to call up and strengthen your psychic powers.

Correspondences and Ingredients

Day: Monday (the Moon)

Candle Color: Lavender (preferred color), blue (the Moon)

Moon Phase: Waxing, or the dark Moon (connected to divination)

The Base: Olive oil, vegetable oil, or grape seed oil

The Herbs: **For divination** – strawberry, thyme, valerian, vanilla, yarrow (arrow root); **for prophetic dreams** – jasmine, marigold, mugwort, onion, rose; **to strengthen psychic powers** – bay, celery, cinnamon, eyebright, grass, lemongrass, lavender, marigold, mugwort, rose, anise, thyme, yarrow (arrow root); **to increase psychic awareness** – anise, bay, cinnamon, cloves, gardenia, lemon grass, lilac, marigold, nutmeg, rose, anise, thyme, yarrow (arrow root); **for astral projection** – dittany of Crete, cinnamon, jasmine, sandalwood

My Recipe

3 pinches of lavender

3 pinches of rosemary

3 marigold blossoms

Sex Oil

Sex... it is a topic that dominates our thoughts for a startling proportion of our lives, consuming us with erotic daydreams and fantasies, consuming us with physical passion for a particular person, or consuming us with just the plain ol' natural instinct to breed. Some people may not like to look at sex in this unromantic light, but it's the truth. Mother Nature is all about procreation. From a magickal perspective, sex oil can be used to tickle someone else's fancy for you, to get things moving at a faster pace when there's a mutual attraction, but also shyness or hesitation. It can be used to increase passion in an already existing relationship. It can be used to give you a breathy, erotic, sexual "glow" that will attract lovers in general (be careful if you take this route); or it can be used to celebrate your own sexuality solo.

Carve your name and the name of the one you desire on a red candle. Anoint this candle with sex oil and perhaps some of your own bodily sexual secretions or saliva, or secretions from the target if you have access to this type of "personal concerns". (This is the earthy hoodoo/voodoo aspect of magick coming to the fore). This oil can be made to accommodate a monogamous couple, instilled with herbs to maintain fidelity; but this is also an area where you want to seriously consider any magickal repercussions that might rear up in the future. The old adage "nothing lasts forever" often proves just too true in romantic relationships. If your relationship with Prince Charming doesn't work out, do you really want to be tied to him physically through a potent magickal bond? You might want to think on this, and you might want to keep things light and general, relying on the universe and lots of stuff you don't know about brewing in the ether world! Someone really cool might be just waiting for you out there, someone you'd never thought of, from somewhere you never imagined.

Gotta love the idea of Love!

Correspondences and Ingredients

Day: Friday (Venus)

Candle Color: Red

Moon Phase: Waxing to full

The Base: Almond oil (preferred); olive oil; and as always – something cheaper if you're pinching pennies

The Herbs: **Fidelity** – chili pepper, clover, cumin, nutmeg, rhubarb; **Lust** (to increase) – celery, cinnamon, daisy, dill, garlic, ginseng, lemon grass, mint, onion, patchouli, rosemary; **Love** – apple, aster, lemon balm, basil, cardamom, catnip, chamomile, cinnamon, cloves, coriander, daisy, dill, gardenia, geranium, ginger, ginseng, jasmine, lavender, marjoram, pansy, rose, rosemary, thyme, valerian, vanilla; **Sexual Potency** (to regain/maintain) – banana, beans, dragon's blood

My Recipe
Fidelity: Cumin, nutmeg rhubarb
Love: Rose, cardamom, cinnamon
Lust: Ginseng, rosemary, patchouli

Prosperity Oil

Money is the center of our existence. And wait, before you raise your hand to disagree, to list all the other things in life more important than, more noble than, money and its acquisition... think about it. Personally, I don't want to live without groceries and electricity, both of which require money to purchase. So when we speak of "Money Magic" and "Prosperity Spells", we're not being big ol' greedy pagans looking for million dollar mansions and stretch limos. Most of us just want to be able to take care of our families, to provide for their basic needs, to live a normal comfortable life. Period.

In order to do this, in the ever-so-human competitive and commercial world out there, we might need a little magickal boost once in a while. And that's where this oil will come in handy. Use it to dress candles used in money spells; use it to anoint talismans for magickal prosperity, energizing stones that you carry in your purse, wallet, or pocket; use it to anoint a special coin etc.

Use your imagination. What's important to you? What do you *need* this money for? To pay your electric bill? Anoint a light bulb with prosperity oil. There are a gazillion ways you can pass on magickal energy to draw money and prosperity to inanimate objects and people. *Put it where you need it most.* Let your instinct and your ingenuity be your guide.

Correspondences and Ingredients

Day: Thursday (Jupiter)
Candle Color: Purple, gold, silver
Moon Phase: Waxing/full
The Base: Olive oil, or as usual, whatever you might have on hand
The Herbs: **Wealth (to obtain)** – allspice, basil, chamomile, cinnamon, cloves, dill, ginger, marjoram, mint, patchouli, pine; **Prosperity** – nuts, oak, tomato, tulip, alfalfa

My Recipe
3 pinches each of patchouli, mint, and dill
1 teaspoon of Drawing Powder (aka powdered sugar)

Summoning Powder

When the witch requests your presence with the wiggle of her pretty little finger, and she uses Summoning Powder to strengthen her will and weaken yours, you will come to her. You might be a little "fuzzy" as to why you feel the sudden urgent need to call this person, or to show up on their doorstep, but you won't be able to resist the inexplicable overpowering pull to do so.

This is how it works; Summoning Powder does just what its name implies. It summons someone to you.

Be gentle, dear witches. Take into consideration that the target of this magick will most definitely be a little discombobulated. They may be honestly puzzled at the situation, feeling out-of-sync with themselves and their surroundings. Ease them into it. When they make that phone call, or knock at your door, comfort them, reassure them. Let them know that they are right where they are supposed to be and all is well.

Correspondences and Ingredients

Day: Any day convenient to you, depending upon the urgency of the matter

Candle Colors: White

Moon Phase: Waxing (of course, to *bring* someone to you)

The Base: Since this is a powder, there will be no oil base

Main Ingredient: The main ingredient in Summoning Powder is incredibly simple – powdered sugar. Don't be duped into spending big bucks on "summoning powder", when you can purchase this item in your local grocery store. (Unless the big bucks you're spending on a batch of summoning powder is actually paying for very pretty and unique packaging!)

The Herbs: You don't have to add any herbs to Summoning Powder, but you can, if you feel a magickal pull to do so – **Rosemary**, to draw someone from your childhood past; **Cardamom**, to draw someone with romantic intentions; **Sage**, to draw someone with whom you need to clear the air; **Mint,** to draw someone for financial reasons; **Ginger**, to draw them quickly.

My Recipe

Just plain powdered sugar – sweet and to the point. Like drawing flies to honey.

Black Cat Oil

Black Cat Oil is a traditional old voodoo oil with historical roots set in New Orleans. It's steeped in mystery and magick, believed to break bad hexes and curses and any other dark 'n' dirty mojo someone might have sent your way. It's also used to draw in love; and it's used to draw in spirits. Its most intriguing and magickal energy comes from the primary ingredient: hair from a black cat.

If you make this oil, and you need to collect hair from a black cat, make sure that you do so without harming the cat! This is so important; I can't emphasize it enough. Black cats, long associated throughout history with witches and witchcraft, magick and the dark arts, have suffered abuse and death at the hands of misinformed, ignorant, frightened individuals. But the really fascinating aspect of black cats is that they are a favorite form for shape-shifting spirits. They are a powerful conduit of magick, and harming these creatures can bring down negative energy and repercussions to the perpetrator in ways that would boggle the mind.

And besides all that, we love our kitty-cats. We want to nourish and care for them, spoil them, and keep them safe. A pox upon anyone who would harm a cat, sez I.

Correspondences and Ingredients

Day: **Monday** (the Moon) – to draw in spirits, to facilitate spirit contact; **Friday** (Venus) – for love and passion; **Saturday** (Saturn) – to break hexes and curses, to return-to-sender negative energy

Candle Colors: Monday: Blue; Friday: Red; Saturday: Black

Moon Phase: Waxing (to draw in love or spirits); waning (to banish dark and negative magick)

The Base: Almond oil (to draw love); grapeseed oil (to draw spirits); castor oil (to break hexes and other bad mojo)

The Herbs: Sage, bay leaves, myrrh

My Recipe
Sage
Bay leaves
Myrrh
The correct oil for the intention
Steel wool
An iron nail
Hair from a black cat

Four Thieves Vinegar

The legend of Four Thieves Vinegar originates with the Middle Ages and the tragedy of the Black Death. As the story goes, there were four looters who seemed to be immune to the plague, going merrily along their way, robbing from homes that had been plague infested, looting from the dead and decaying bodies of its victims, with no harm to themselves. Their secret, so the story goes, is a special recipe, a vinegar, which they either ingested and/or anointed themselves with... "Four Thieves Vinegar".

Besides being used to banish illness, this magickal concoction is a crucial component in many banishing and commanding spells. This vinegar is also excellent for banishing unwanted people in your life, so use with discretion and care. There are two versions to the recipe – one is edible, one is not. Since I don't like the smell of it, have no intention of ingesting it, and use it for a variety of magick, most of which has nothing to do with healing illness... *my recipe is not edible.* I repeat, do not ingest what you create with my recipe.

Okay then, now that we're clear on that.

Correspondences and Ingredients

Day: **Sunday** (the Sun) – for healing; **Saturday** (Saturn) – for banishing; **Tuesday** (Mars) – for controlling commanding spells

Candle Color: **Sunday:** White; **Saturday:** Black; **Tuesday:** Orange

Moon Phase: Waning, to banish; waxing, to bring something about

The Base: Red wine, or apple cider vinegar

The Herbs: Four of any of the following – garlic, black pepper, coriander, lavender, mint, rosemary, rue, sage, thyme, wormwood[8]

My Recipe
The base: Apple-cider vinegar
4 garlic cloves

sage
thyme
wormwood
black pepper

Graveyard Dirt

Cemetery dirt, it's special. It's not like soil found anywhere else, and the reason for this is that it is blessed, consecrated, sacred. It is an incredibly powerful magickal tool that can be used to great advantage in so many versatile ways. First, graveyard dirt isn't just graveyard dirt in general. You can get so much more specific than that. You are ill, or a loved one is sick, and you need a healing? If you want to use this ingredient in healing magick, don't just drive out to your local cemetery, stop along any lane, and scoop up a handful of soil. Think... you need healing, you need to restore good health. *You need a physician.* You'll want to find the grave of a doctor. When you do, you'll want to approach the grave with reverence and respect. Communicate with the spirit whose grave this is; ask for their blessing; ask for their help; and *thank them.* This gentle soul, dedicated to healing when they were alive, will most certainly continue to aide in healing from the other side. This applies to any other magick as well. Money issues? You'll want a banker. Protection? A close relative who would've defended you in life will defend you yet, from the other side.

The only other etiquette that I follow when gathering anything from a cemetery, is to leave behind a silver coin, as payment for services rendered, as a magickal token of my gratitude.

Banishing Oil

Banishing oils are generally used in banishing spells, whether you're trying to rid yourself of undesirable people, situations, habits, or things. Just make sure that what you think you want banished, you really do. Getting something back is much more work than making something go away. And if you really want something to go away, and you want it to go away in a timely fashion, make sure that you correlate your spell-crafting, and the use of this oil, with the correct moon phase for just such endeavors.

Correspondences and Ingredients

Day: Saturn

Candle Color: Black

Moon Phase: Waning, or the dark moon

The Base: Castor oil (preferred), but use whatever is available to you

The Herbs: Black pepper, cayenne pepper, cinnamon, cloves

Extra Ingredients: sea salt and sulpher

My Recipe
Castor oil
Black pepper
Cayenne pepper
Cinnamon
Sea salt
Sulpher
"Personal concerns" from the target, if possible, or a snatch of something connected to the issue or object to be banished

Command and Compel Oil

"Commanding Oil" is generally used in binding spells, to get an individual to bend to your will and do what you want, or to gain control of a situation. This oil has a strong history in voodoo and New Orleans hoodoo culture and is used almost exclusively to exert your will over others. The most common method for using this oil consists of candle magick, with a candle to represent yourself (white), and a candle to represent the target (black). Dress the target's candle in this oil, adding any symbols or such that you feel might be relevant to the target, or the situation. Likewise, name the candle representing yourself. You could add your astrological sign, birthdate, and such, to personalize it greatly, highlighting the connection, revving up the energy.

The most important idea to this process is that you set the candles up with the candle representing yourself raised *above* the target's candle. Personally, I'd go to town on a spell like this. If you're going to do something this magickally drastic, you might as well do it in a big way that's going to carry lots of punch: set it all up on an altar. If the main difficulty here is money, then use this theme in your altar decorations. If the problem is love, there you go. You'll want to incorporate images and items on the altar that correspond to whatever it is that's got your goat. And this is how you do it, and do it good.

Correspondences and Ingredients

Day: **Monday**: Female issues – or targets, figurative obstacles; **Tuesday**: Marriage, enemies, physical obstacles; **Wednesdays**: Mental obstacles, targets adding to your mental stress, people you just can't get through to with normal communication; **Thursday**: Business and legal issues, and those individuals or people connected to the topic; **Friday**: Love – in all its aspects, here's where you bring out the big gun as far as relationships go and getting what you want (just be careful what you wish for); **Saturday**: All the nasties, this is the day to bring down enemies and the bad guys and regain control of your life (the universe will be listening now); **Sunday**: Male issues... is there a man you need to control, but none of the above situations seem to apply?...catch him here.

Candle Color: Black and white[9]

Moon Phase: Waning, of course, and the third quarter moon, when it's half-way to the dark moon (a mid-way point, a threshold) is actually the most powerful time to do this magick

The Base: Castor oil is good, but any oil will do the trick,

"Witches' Oil" is even better

The Herbs: Sweet flag (aka calamus root), licorice root... grind them into a powder and add to your oil; bergamot can be added specifically for financial issues

My Recipe
Witches' Oil
Calamus root
Licorice root

Uncrossing Oil

This oil is most often used to remove hexes, curses, or any other bad mojo you believe has been cast against you. It's also brought into service to turn bad luck around and is used in spells for just such results. It's the magickal oil you need to cast negative energy away from you, to cleanse your space, your magickal essence, and your head. I've been contacted by people who were so freaked out just at the thought that someone *might* have hexed them in some way that they had become panic stricken. They were so freaked out, in fact, that they were becoming their own worst enemy and doing more damage to themselves than any enemy could intentionally inflict.

If you feel that someone is messing with you through witch-craft or voodoo, first – don't panic, really. Know that you can fix this. The power is within you, and the power is within this oil. Everything will be okay. You might even get the last laugh.

Correspondences and Ingredients

Day: Any day will do, Saturday is best, but if you're feeling swallowed up by something nasty, best get rid of it quickly
Candle Color: Black
Moon Phase: Waning, but again, in an emergency do what you have to do when you have to do it
The Base: Castor oil, with a dash of jojoba oil to make it thinner

The Herbs: Hyssop, angelica, frankincense, black pepper, cayenne
pepper, a sprig of rue, a sliver of fresh garlic

Other ingredients: Sea salt, a section of broken chain

Note: The two most crucial ingredients here are the *hyssop* and the
broken chain, everything else listed is to be added as desired, at
your own discretion. The easiest and most accessible chain
I've used is a dainty jewelry chain. Remember, they must be
broken (it's all in the symbolism), so take a necklace or
bracelet chain and snap off a section for your Uncrossing Oil.

My Recipe
Hyssop
Broken chain
Sea salt,
Sliver of garlic
Frankincense

Endnotes

1. This quote is words from the song "Proud Mary", by Tina Turner.
2. Except for minor corrections for spelling or punctuation and minimal editing, all of the contributions sent to me have been published "as is".
3. The timeline for the "Thresholds" is generalized. Each woman is unique and so is her experience.
4. Major Arcana is from *The Motherpeace Tarot Deck*.
5. Correspondences for days of the week are tightly tied to the planets. It would be repetitive to include those correspondences here, so take a peek at Days of the Week for more info.
6. Next Millennium, the ultimate shop for new-age magickal items: **www.next-mill.com**.
7. "Dressing" a candle simply means to anoint it with a magickal oil and roll it in the appropriate herbs for your intentions. You might also choose to carve a name or appropriate symbols in your candle as well.
8. Wormwood is **poisonous**... Do Not Ingest!
9. See correspondences in Days of the Week if this will pertain more closely to your situation or issue.

Other Books by Amythyst Raine (Hatayama)

Tarot: A Witch's Journey, Labyrinth House, 2010

The Gray Witch's Grimoire, Moon Books, JHP, 2012

Tarot for Grownups, Dodona Books, JHP, 2013

For more info and links: **ladyamythyst.com**
Amythyst's books can also be purchased at:
Next Millennium
3141 N. 93rd St.
Omaha, Nebraska 68134
Phone: 402 393-1126
www.next-mill.com/

Websites and Blogs

Every Cat Has a Tale is her personal blog spot, which includes everyday life, dilemmas, as well as victories, memoirs, opinions, maybe a rare rant now and then, along with inspiration for mundane life, personal photos, and videos:
everycathasatale.blogspot.com

Magickal Connections is her very popular witchy, pagan, booky blog spot: **wytchymystique.com**

The Witch's Corner is her very popular witchy pagan website full of witchy pagan stuff: **ladyamythyst.com**

Tarot Readings with Amythyst Raine

Amythyst Raine-Hatayama is a psychic/clairvoyant who gives kick-ass tarot readings using the intuitive method. These readings reveal your past, explore your future and, more often than not, connect you to the spirit world.

She gives personal private readings in her home (by appointment only), as well as locally in Fremont NE and the Omaha/Metro area. She also gives readings by phone, email, Skype, and video; as well as readings for parties, corporate events, shops, and bookstores.

For more information, follow this link:

tarotreadingswithamythystraine.blogspot.com

Moon Books invites you to begin or deepen your encounter with
Paganism, in all its rich, creative, flourishing forms.